Retire
with
Confidence

Your Toolbox
for
Financial Independence

by Gregory Luken

Library of Congress Control Number: 2005909068
    Luken, Gregory.
        Retire with confidence : your toolbox for financial
    independence / by Gregory Luken.
        p. cm.
        ISBN 09772698-6-8

        1. Retirement income--United States--Planning.
    2. Retirees--United States--Finance, Personal. 3. Baby
    boom generation--United States--Finance, Personal.
    I. Title.

    HG179.L847 2006   332.024'014
                                   QBI05-600167

Cover design by Brad Talbott
Interior layout by Julie Rust

For more information: www.retiringconfident.com

Published by:
Yale Hammersmith Publishing
1894 Gen. George Patton
Suite 500
Franklin, TN 37067

Printed in the United States of America.

ACKNOWLEDGMENTS

I would like to thank the following people for their effort and contribution in transforming this work from a thought into a book:

Jeff Bradford for his thoughtful work on editing; Ann Boyd for her proofreading and suggestions on keeping it real; Mike DeRosa and the SII team for your input; Julie Rust for her work on layout; Brad Talbott for the cover design; to all my family and friends for encouraging me along the way. And mom and dad -- thanks for everything.

TABLE OF CONTENTS

Introduction
GETTING STARTED

Think Income

At a time when the largest generation in American history is preparing to face retirement, we find that we've spent most of our investing lives learning how to **grow** our money. Now it's time to think **income**. The fact is some of the things that worked during the growth stage will be counterproductive during the income stage. It's time to adjust our approach if we hope to enjoy our retirement rather than simply endure it.

This book is about that change. There are many books on growing your money, day trading and getting rich quick. This isn't one of those. I wrote this book to help you <u>understand</u> some guiding principles for protecting your wealth in order to generate a growing income stream in retirement. It is my hope that this book will be more than a source of valuable information. I hope it will help *you* overcome the challenges ahead, distinguish between good and bad investment information, and show you how to transform information into knowledge so that you can take decisive action.

The Boomer Challenge

You are facing a challenge today that Americans have never encountered. The last time a generation had to take so much personal responsibility for their financial well-being late in life, the typical expected lifespan was less than 50 years. Your parents and grandparents could rely on government and corporate caretakers to manage the risk of building and maintaining their retirement income. No more. This responsibility has shifted back to you. Social Security cannot remain in its current state. Fewer and fewer companies offer lifetime pensions. Equity investments are not the 'sure thing' they seemed to be in the late 20th Century and the world is not the same: globalization has made markets more complex.

How To Read This Book

↗ <u>**Retirement Reality Check**</u>: Allows you to hit the highlights in under an hour.

↘ <u>**It's Like This**</u>: Important concepts are restated in ways you might find more interesting and useful – even entertaining.

☞ <u>**What Dad Said**</u>: Whether it was teaching school or running an auto dealership, my father always seemed to be able see to the heart of things. These insights have been invaluable to me. Perhaps they will to you, too.

✐ <u>**Can You Imagine**</u>: Examples of how average investors approach retirement planning. These vignettes, hypothetical in nature, help put a face on how the principles outlined could affect your neighbors, your friends or even your family.

If You Only Have 10 Minutes

This book is designed so that it can be read in 1) 10 minutes, 2) about an hour or 3) four hours or more. If you only have 10 minutes to spare, you can understand the gist of this book by reading the chapter summaries below. You won't find all the answers here, but you may find the questions you need to ask yourself. (And you may realize that you probably can afford to invest and hour or more to get the whole story).

1. Time To Take The Shades Off (Facing Reality)

Boomers are facing a confluence of trends that will make it more difficult to retire than it was for their parents: fewer pensions, a precarious Social Security system, extended life expectancies, a stagnant stock market, globalization, inflation and more. Yet, for too many of us, hope is our only strategy for funding retirement. Others, who are trying to prepare, may be asking the wrong questions. But there is a solution. It requires 1) Knowledge (not just raw information), 2) Decisive Action (not just planning) and 3) Realistic Expectations (requiring objectivity and humility.)

2. The George Burns Syndrome (Preparing for a Longer Life)

Statistics can be factually and statistically correct yet lead us to believe a lie with mortal ramifications. Statistically, as of 2001, the average life expectancy of an American is 77.2 years.[1] In reality, as you are probably aware from personal experience, people are living longer today (even on average) than they did a generation or two ago. In reality, we are lying to ourselves by planning on a retirement that lasts until age 75. To be safe and realistic, we should be planning for a retirement that may reach to age 95 or 100. Even if you don't live this long, it's quite possible that your partner will. What will happen to your spouse for the last 20-25 years of his or her life if your retirement savings are exhausted at age 75?

3. The Postage Stamp Syndrome (Dealing with Inflation)
The postage stamp is a proxy for the ravages of inflation. In 1974, a first class postage stamp was 10 cents. Today it is 37 cents and soon will increase to 42 cents. You may need an income stream that will triple during retirement. Underestimating this risk could leave you with a stable income but with diminishing purchasing power, effectively making you poorer each year.

4. Disinheriting Your Uncle Sam (Dealing with Taxes)
As you think about saving and investing for retirement, imagine a bucket you are working to fill. At retirement, you will live on what's in the bucket. Obviously, not only do you want your bucket to be full, but you want to assure it's a sound bucket with no leaks. Taxes are a hole in your bucket that can drain or wipe out your efforts to fill it. You want to plug as many of these holes as you can so your bucket is still full when you retire.

5. Risk and Return (Understanding the Market)
Because you may live longer than the 'average' life span and thus be exposed to inflation for longer periods of time than previous generations, you need assets that have the potential to grow with or above the rate of inflation. Equity markets are an excellent choice in this regard. However, equity strategies that work well during the accumulation phase of your retirement plan can undermine or wipe out your savings during the income phase. Different parts of the market behave differently and you must have a strategy to deal with the often erratic behavior of different types of investments, such as small company stocks, blue chip stocks and foreign stocks. Over long periods of time, the large company stock index has averaged about 10%. In the short term, however, market returns very rarely fall in the 8-12% range.[2] So, while returns may be greater with equities than many other assets over the long

haul, that is little consolation when you are depending on your investment income to pay the grocery bill every month. At that time of your life, it is essential that your investment strategies be geared to income instead of growth.

6. Taking Care of Care Taking (Confronting Long-Term Health Care)

Sixty years ago people didn't think about nursing homes or assisted living facilities because they didn't exist. Today people are living longer and may need some form of assistance late in life, either at home or in a skilled care facility. There is a tremendous risk – about a 50% probability – that at least one person from a married couple age 65 today will need long-term care in his or her later years. And this kind of care is very expensive, as much as $50,000 to $90,000 a year in today's dollars. For many people, an additional expense of this magnitude could devastate their retirement savings. Yet sadly, most people are self-insuring, assuming 100% of the risk themselves, rather than reinsuring and spreading the risk for just pennies on the dollar.

7. The Ostrich Syndrome (Understanding the Need to Begin Planning Now)

When it comes to investing, time is your best friend. When it comes to planning, time is your worst enemy. Given the complexity of life, the shifting tax codes, investment volatility, estate tax law changes and a myriad of other factors, many find themselves in a state of financial paralysis when it comes to planning. Difficult as it may be, we must resist the temptation to stick our heads in the sand and simply avoid thinking about the whole matter. Failure to plan is planning to fail. It's that simple.

8. The Roadmap (Creating a Plan and Its Value to You)

If you planned to travel to Los Angeles by car, you would do several things. You would make sure you had a vehicle that would get you there. You might even get your oil changed and have the belts, hoses and fluids checked. Although you may not expect to have a flat tire, you would probably make sure you had a good spare tire on board. And you would also have a map to assure that you head in the right direction - and that you are able to find an alternate route should road construction require you to take a detour. Financially speaking, it makes sense to do the same thing. A financial roadmap won't keep detours from occurring, but it will help you get to your destination if they arise.

1- National Center for Health Statistics, Centers for Disease Control, 2005.

2 - Standard & Poor's market data, 2005

Chapter 1
TIME TO TAKE THE SHADES OFF

Is This For You?

Will you ever be able to retire? How do you know if you can afford to retire? How much income will you need when you retire? What about ten years later? Can you afford to *stay* retired? How long will you need the income? What if you have healthcare needs along the way? These are some of the issues we'll be dealing with in a straightforward manner.

If you are looking for a manual on how to become a day trader, how to get rich speculating on foreign currency markets or a snake oil manual on how to make 50% returns every year, then you've picked up the wrong book. If you're under 30 years old, just getting started financially, or trying to get debt under control, there's much more relevant content for you to read elsewhere.

This is for the reader who has accumulated wealth and wants to retire in the next 10 years or so, or for those already retired. Our focus is how to take what has been accumulated and convert it into a comfortable lifestyle in retirement. We'll deal with the special demands and stress placed on an income portfolio, which are much different than those you faced in accumulating and growing your retirement fund. We'll explore some guiding principles for saving your money – and protecting it – in order to generate a growing income stream in retirement. And we'll try to keep it fun along the way!

This is not intended to be a complete do-it-yourself manual. Rather, it is designed to convey essential concepts that will help you be a more insightful, thoughtful and successful investor so you can live the life you want to live. As we move through the text, we'll dispel some of the myths, clear up some misconceptions and help you avoid some of the mistakes that plague many people today.

From what I've seen in our workshops and seminars and heard from people coming into our office, I am painfully aware that some of the people who need this information the most are the same people who won't get past this page - if they even open the cover. But for those who are open, it is my sincere desire

1

that this book helps to close the disconnect between perception and reality about retirement income.

Thank you for reading this book. I hope you enjoy it and that it makes a difference in your life.

▄◄ WHAT DAD SAID ▶▄

What Really Matters

Growing up in Kentucky, I remember my dad not only telling me, but showing me with the example of his life, one of the core values he worked to instill in me.

Whatever you do in life, he said and showed, focus on what you can do for other people. That is my desire with this text. If it gives you an intellectual understanding of these concepts but fails to inspire any action, then it's been a failure.

It is my hope that this book will be more than a source of valuable information. I hope it will help you distinguish between good and bad information, then how to transform information into knowledge, and finally how to make good decisions based on your knowledge.

I also hope this book will enable you to ask the right questions. Have you ever visited your doctor only to return home thinking about all the things you should've asked? Family members may have asked you about this and that and you didn't know the answer. You may have wondered what you need to know to be a savvy patient. Perhaps you've visited an advisor and had a similar experience. You made some decisions, but weren't entirely clear by the time you got home about exactly what was going on. Hopefully, after reading this book, this won't happen again.

Getting Started

How do you create an income stream that will last a lifetime and maintain your standard of living? How do you secure a worry-free retirement without compromising your current lifestyle?

You are facing challenges today that Americans have not faced for many generations. The good news is people are living longer, living healthier and are more active later in life than they've ever been. The bad news is that because people are living longer there is a mounting financial crisis. Many people – thousands who think they're okay today – may have incomes that expire before they do.

There is a confluence of forces at work: a population that's living longer than any generation in history, the hardly perceptible erosion of purchasing power by inflation, low interest rates, increased stock market volatility, a Social Security System that cannot be sustained in its current status and fewer employer sponsored pensions and healthcare benefits in retirement.

All this is transpiring just as the largest generation in the history of this country is beginning to retire. Although the effects aren't visible today, these forces are welling up like a tidal wave in the middle of the ocean. The effects on the shore aren't seen until the forces converge there. And then it's too late.

Almost everyone getting ready to retire has enough money to last until next Friday. The challenge is making sure that you have enough money 20, 30, even 40 years into retirement.

Thousands of Americans face this challenge today as they transition into a new phase of their investing lives. While some basic principals remain the same, many of the investment rules and methodologies must change as we move from the *growth* (or accumulation) *phase* to the *spending phase*. This is a significant change and change is hard. Just ask any dinosaur.

Of course, you can't ask a dinosaur anything, can you? They suffered the ultimate consequence of not changing. They probably hoped things would get better.

We can't afford to behave like financial dinosaurs: trapped in a dangerous state of financial paralysis and not taking the necessary steps to plan for our financial futures. Simply hoping.

 **It's Like This**

TENDING OUR FINANCIAL GARDEN

In many ways, taking care of your money is like tending a garden. We know that whatever we plant is what will grow. We're not going to plant apples and harvest oranges. And we know that every seed we plant will not have an equal yield to the other seeds. We plant, we water, we weed and fertilize and ultimately we let the inevitable laws of nature take effect.

While we can't control the outcome, we can certainly manage the environment to affect the outcome. When the dry season comes, we can make sure we provide plenty of water. When weeds sprout up we can remove them. We can properly till the soil. We can fertilize. We can do many things to try to ensure the best crop possible.

What we don't do is also very important. We don't plant a seed and go out 24 hours later to dig the seed up to see if it's sprouting. A good gardener also doesn't plant a good seed and forget about it. Doing so would provide a very predictable yield – chaos.

A good gardener prunes to maximize the yield. That means skillfully cutting not only dead or dying parts of the plant, but often good, green and growing parts in a way that doesn't destroy the plant but increases the desired result.

Great portfolios should be tended with the same degree of care, knowledge, diligence and discipline as a great garden.

We each have a choice. We can simply hope that everything will be okay. Or, we can confront the situation and by understanding it we can create the solution, improve our probabilities, and avoid costly mistakes. And that's a real reason for hope!

The Three Stages of Your Investment Life

Growth Stage. This is the accumulation phase where you save and invest to build your retirement fund. It's the "getting" stage and starts when you start saving money. Investment earnings are plowed back into investments to further compound returns. After you retire you might still have some money invested for growth. But the primary objective of the growth stage is to accumulate and increase wealth.

Income Stage. When you get to the point where you are spending income out of your retirement fund, you are in the income stage. This is what we traditionally think of as "retirement." This phase starts when income from our business or profession begins to taper off or stop. <u>This is the stage we will concentrate on in this book</u>.

Legacy Stage. The Legacy stage is where you begin the process of giving or passing along the wealth that you can't take with you. This is also called the Transference stage or Estate Planning.

These stages or phases frequently overlap and sometimes you may have all three taking place at the same time. The rules, strategies and tactics differ in each stage. What may work well when you're growing your assets may lead to disaster when you begin taking income. What's tax efficient for you

---

✓   R E T I R E M E N T   R E A L I T Y   C H E C K   🔨

Plan Vs. Hope
When you get right down to it, you either have a plan or you have a bet. A plan is a process that has been tested and accounts for problems before they arise. A bet is simply hoping that you will win. Hope is a wonderful thing. It sustains us when things look bleak. It gives us the strength to fight another day. But hope is not a strategy.

may not be tax efficient to your heirs. We tend to make the biggest financial mistakes when we assume that the way things worked in one stage is the way they'll work in the next.

The Most Critical Stage

In my opinion, the financial services industry has done a pretty good job of educating investors about the growth phase. But little has been done in preparing investors – or even advisors – to adequately handle the retirement income challenge.

If you make a mistake or mess up early in the growth phase it can be relatively easy to recover. Let's say you don't contribute the legal limit to your 401(k), IRAs or other retirement plans, or you take some wild risks, or even cash out of the market at the wrong time - you may still have years or decades to make up for lost time. Early mistakes are easier to fix.

If you make mistakes in the transference stage you may cause problems for your spouse, your kids or your grandkids and end up giving thousands of dollars to your Uncle Sam that could have gone to the people and causes you really care about. But if all this happens after you depart from this mortal coil, you can argue that you won't be around so it's not really your problem. (Of course, it might be pointed out that you weren't very prudent in caring for your family. But, that's for another book.)

A mistake in the income phase is different; it could jeopardize your lifestyle for the rest of your life as well as your legacy. An income phase mistake can have an impact on your income every month for the rest of your days.

✓	RETIREMENT REALITY CHECK	⌐

Three Keys to a Successful Retirement:
1. Knowledge: Information is just raw data that has not been turned into something applicable to your life. Knowledge is something you can effectively use.
2. Decisive Action: Making a good decision, which requires knowledge, is one thing. Acting on it, which requires discipline, is another.
3. Realistic Expectations: This requires humility and objectivity, two traits that don't come easy. But, with practice, you can acquire them – and be much happier, not just wealthier.

The Retirement Income Crisis

Most of us invest so much time and energy growing our portfolios – the growth stage is usually the longest - that our thinking can get stuck in a growth mode. We must learn to think of the income phase of our lives as not just more of the same. It may have been easy to be lulled into complacency by the curse of the good times in the 1990s and believe that a $1 million portfolio should give a $100,000 current lifestyle indefinitely. A rude awakening may be on the horizon even if investments do earn 10% on average. The time to address it is now.

By understanding where we've been and where we want to go we can get a grasp on how to appropriately deal with the situation at hand. Let's look at some of the major issues so we can get it right the first time.

Asking the Right Questions

Have you ever climbed up a ladder and gotten to the top rung only to find the ladder was leaning against the wrong wall? I have.

When I went to work in my first job after college, it occurred to me that the questions were no longer provided for me. For 16 years of schooling, teachers had provided the questions and all I had to do was figure out the

---

✎ It's Like This

Rubik's Cube

Do you remember 'Rubik's Cube?' The Rubik's Cube was a three dimensional puzzle with nine colored squares on each face. The goal was to get all the squares lined up so that each of the six faces of the cube was the same color. And you couldn't move just one square; you had to move an entire row or column at a time. Every time you moved a piece of the cube, it affected the squares all the way around the cube.

Financial planning – investing for retirement, your kids' and grandkids' education, retirement income and estate planning –is very much like Rubik's Cube: when you move one piece it can affect the rest of the pieces.

The focus for our time together is to meet the challenge of having a comfortable, worry-free retirement without getting derailed by the things that could jeopardize that income, lifestyle and ultimately your peace of mind. How do we make sure that stock market declines, rising costs, medical issues and unexpected expenses don't sidetrack our plans?

I have seen so many financial mistakes over the years. I've made a ton myself. We all make mistakes, but successful people learn from their mistakes. In this book, I'm going to share with you some of the key mistakes often experienced by others so that you have the opportunity to learn from them. So that your attempts to fix part of your investment Rubik's Cube doesn't end up causing problems elsewhere.

answer. Now I had to first figure out the right question, too. Frequently in life, we spend time and energy getting the right answer only to figure out too late that we were answering the wrong question.

Let me illustrate. Suppose I told you Tom Coley is a fishmonger. Tom is 5'11" tall. He wears a size 12 1/2 shoe, has a 37" waist and his neck measures 17 1/2". What does Tom Coley weigh?

It's easy to spend a lot of energy and time focusing on the wrong thing when the reality is right in front of you. In the case of Mr. Coley, you might ask if he's skinny or heavy. Someone might guess he weighs 235 pounds based on someone they know who is about Tom's size. But, they'd be grasping for the right answer to the wrong question. Since Tom Coley is a fishmonger, he of course weighs fish.

Financially speaking, some people think the question is *how much* Tom weighs when the question is really *what* Tom weighs.

Fewer Pensions

The responsibility for funding retirement is shifting from the corporate world to you. Today, fewer and fewer people are covered by healthcare benefits after retirement and a shrinking number of people have pension benefits. For every four defined benefit pension plans in existence in 1985, there was just one in 2003[1]. Both retirement and employee medical benefit programs are shifting more and more responsibility to the individual.

A generation or two ago it was not uncommon to work for a company for 30 years and retire with a lifetime pension and healthcare benefits and then live 10 or 15 years in retirement. With our lifespan increasing, many people will be faced with the question of how to finance a lifetime that's lasting longer than most of us thought was possible against the backdrop of continuously increasing costs.

✓   RETIREMENT REALITY CHECK   ↖

Decisive Action
We can spend a lot of time working on the "right answer" to the wrong question. When I was a stockbroker I thought people were asking, "How do I get the highest rate of return?" when what they really wanted to know was, "How do I get as much money as I want?" Answer each question correctly and you could get radically different answers.

The Market

Just as the Great Depression and the brutal bear market of 1973-74 left its mark on an earlier generation, the recent bear market of 2000-2002 has left its claw marks on the psychology, lives and pocketbooks of a generation. Many people have had to adjust their budgets, downsize their expectations and delay their plans for retirement because of the major financial setback they suffered. Some have even gone back to work. Surely you know or have heard people say they thought they'd be able to retire a couple of years ago. Now they plan on working another decade. This last bear market has brought home the daunting challenge of funding a comfortable retirement.

There is a silver lining to this recent bear market. By creating the 'problem' (or more accurately, helping people realize the reality that was there all along) early in the cycle of retiring Boomers, it may have averted disastrous financial consequences for us as a nation. Having a market melt-down and seeing your 401(k) turned into a 201(k) (that's what happens when you lose half of your money) is something you may be able to recover from at age 50. It may not be comfortable or fun and most likely will be very painful, but it's not the end of the world. However, at 70, it's not something from which one could likely recover.

The Baby Boom Generation

The Baby Boom Generation is generally noted as people born between 1946 and 1964. Because of the tremendous size of this generation it's frequently referred to as a football moving through the belly of a snake – it is a giant bulge in population. I believe the important principal to understand is that *the world has never been prepared* for the changes this generation has brought about.

✓   **RETIREMENT REALITY CHECK**   ⌐

Knowledge

"...in just 14 years we will begin paying more in benefits than we collect in taxes. Without changes, by 2042 the Social Security Trust Fund will be exhausted." – *Social Security Administration Report (2004)*

In the 1950s there was a shortage of schools. In the 1960s, as Boomers reached peak "rebellion age," social protests reached new heights. As boomers aged and entered the workforce en masse in the 1970s, a shortage of offices created tremendous demand for commercial real estate and debt financing. Increased demand for money helped keep interest rates high. During the 1980s, developers couldn't build shopping malls fast enough and demand for European cars and wine surged as their careers moved solidly ahead. By the 1990s, the men of the generation had started their midlife crisis. And what was their cure? A b-i-g bike. The result was that demand for Harley Davidson motorcycles was so great there was frequently a waiting list of months.

Now as Baby Boomers approach retirement we are faced with the specter of seeing America's over-65 population double to more than 70 million people by the year 2040. What changes are likely to occur?

Let's put it another way: over the next 16 years, the over-50 age demographic is expected to grow by 74 percent. The under-50 crowd will grow by about 1 percent.

But the one thing Baby Boomers have in common with prior generations is they will want income during retirement. More people will need investments specifically for income than ever before.

Social *In*security

For those of us willing to accept the reality of simple addition and subtraction, we realize that Social Security in its current form cannot and will not exist too far into the future. Something's got to give.

If you haven't already started drawing Social Security, you get an annual mailing from The Social Security Administration that lists your income for the past several years and your estimated benefits should you start drawing at 62, 65 or 70.

The Social Security Administration is trying to make a point with this mailing. On the front page it reads, "Social Security benefits were not intended to be the only source of income for you and your family when you retire. You'll need to supplement your income from a pension plan, savings or investments." Not too hard to read between the lines there, is it? We need to plan for our own retirement income. Sadly, one in three retirees have all or most of their income coming from Social Security[2].

As I prepared to write this, I asked everyone I met with for a week if they remembered getting one of these statements. Everyone said "yes" and each knew within a few dollars what their estimated income would be. When I asked if they had read the first page, not a single person had. In one of these meetings, which was with a young executive who had the statement with her, I asked her to read part of the first page out loud. "In just 14 years we will begin paying more in benefits than we collect in taxes. Without changes, by 2042 the Social Security Trust Fund will be exhausted." This is on the front page.

Social Security was implemented in the United States in 1935 based on Germany's program, which was established in 1889. People are living longer

☞ CAN YOU IMAGINE: ☜
The Discipline of Selling

Steve was 48-years-old, he had already been "retired" for two and a half decades – more than half of his life and had a 'play' account worth about two million dollars. He owned only a few, very concentrated stock positions. In one of the rallies of the late 1990s, the stock started running up dramatically. In less than 5 years it went from $6 per share to more than $90 per share. When the stock got to a point his advisor thought would be at least a near-term high, he talked Steve into selling some of the stock at $92 1/2.

A few days later, Steve called his advisor short of breath and asked, "Have you seen how XYZ stock is running?" The advisor said, "Yes, but that doesn't change our strategy. Even if it continues up, you still own half of your original position." Steve wanted to stop the diversification strategy he and his advisor had agreed on since his stock was going up so dramatically. And it was, after all, Steve's money.

Steve called back during lunch and spoke to a different member of the advisor's team and instructed them to buy back the stock that he had previously sold.

Steve was right. The stock continued up above $92 1/2. In fact, for a few brief moments it kissed $100 per share. And then the slide began. At $95 on the way down the advisor called Steve about selling half. "No way." He called him again at $87 1/2. "Forget about it. This stock is going to run." He called him again at $82 1/2. "If I wouldn't sell it at $95, why would I sell it at $82 1/2?" At what price would he would consider selling some of this volatile stock? He said "over $100." His advisor asked, "What if it never gets to $100 again?" No answer.

Steve saw $100,000 turn into more than $1,800,000 in less than 5 years. A couple of years later, Steve called in to sell all of that stock that was once worth $1,800,000 for a grand total of $27,000.

The discipline of selling is always the hardest part.

now than they were then. The simple reality is that Social Security will change. How will it change? No one, not even the politicians, knows at this point. But it will change and any change we see under the current administration is not likely to be the last change you will see.

The Big Shift

Psychologists tell us that retiring is one of life's most stressful changes. It is major shift in one's mindset. From an investment standpoint, it is a shift from thinking about growth to thinking about income. What your investment will do over the next 50 years may pale in comparison to your need for grocery money right now.

The transition to the income phase is more than just a move from work to retirement. It requires a major change in the way we think about and manage money.

The income stage places different demands and stress on the portfolio. It requires a higher level of diligence to age-appropriate investing. This new phase of investing will require us to use the best of our technological advancements for managing and reducing risk. Since we can't avoid risk, we have to manage it. The consequences of not making prudent planning and investment decisions can be painful and downright ugly.

It's Not About Intelligence

There are a lot of brilliant people who are broke.

When I started working as a stockbroker at a regional investment firm, there was a man who started about the same time I did. I admired his intelligence. He was so incredibly smart. One day he stood by my desk telling me why a local bank stock was the "buy of the century." He

---

✓ **RETIREMENT REALITY CHECK** 🔨

Knowledge
It's important that we understand how money works and grasp concepts that can help us without getting stuck in the idea that we have to know all the information about something before we can use it. We have to know what is important for our purposes.

understood the balance sheet, he quoted statistics off the income statement and he compared relative book value and thoroughly confused me with facts. You could tell he knew his stuff. He painted a compelling picture. Then I asked him how many clients he had explained this to and how much he owned. Sadly, he didn't own the stock and had only shared the information with two clients. His investment thesis was correct: the bank was subsequently bought out and was a great investment. Of course, he was no longer in the business and only two clients got the benefit of his knowledge. He had massive intelligence, but it wasn't put into action.

It's Not About Having ALL the Information

If all it took to be financially successful was having the most information, then librarians would be the wealthiest people in the world. I've known several librarians in my life - wonderful people, but not the wealthiest.

My seven-year-old nephew knows nothing about cathode ray tubes, computer chips, program-

---

◆ WHAT DAD SAID ◆

Do you want it or not?

I grew up on a dead-end street. All the houses on our side of the street backed up to the Preston farm. I'm sure I spent more time as a kid on that farm than Mr. Preston did. When he was in his 80s he decided to move into town and my dad bought the land behind us. He subdivided it so that there was an extra lot behind each house on our street. He went down the street asking each neighbor if they wanted to buy one lot behind their house so they would be doubling the size of their yard. By doing this, he paid for a sizable portion of the farm he had remaining.

One day I remember walking out to the fence line, my dad leaning on a fence post having a conversation with Mr. Tom who lived down the street. He was a contractor and was the only person on that side of the street who had not bought a lot. When I walked up Mr. Tom was talking about the economy, about new construction and what the government was doing and uncertainty about an economic slowdown. I was probably 13-years-old. I was so impressed listening to this dizzying monologue about the country's economy. My dad listened for a few minutes and then said in an even tone, "Economy up. Economy down. It's been going up and down for as long as I've known. Do you want the property or not?"

I have never forgotten that day. People will always complain about "the economy," "taxes," the "government," "the market," and a thousand other things out of their control. My dad understood looking through all the smoke screens and taking decisive action.

ming language, software or direct current. However, that has not stopped him from becoming an expert at Playstation and X-Box video games and beating me at just about any game we play. He doesn't have all the information but he possesses the critical knowledge needed to win.

Through the use of fiber optic communications, we can now take all the information contained in every quarterly report of every company that has ever been listed on the New York Exchange from its inception and transmit it from New York to Los Angeles in less than two seconds. The question becomes, two seconds later, what do you know? What have you learned?

It's Not About Beating the "Market"

Facing retirement with confidence is not about beating the stock market. It's not even about getting the highest gross rate of return. If the question is "How do I beat the stock market?" you could end up with the right answer to the wrong question.

Have you heard this from an investment company in the last five years? "You've done great! The market is down 30% from it's high and you've only lost 29% (of everything you've work hard all your life for and were hoping to retire on and send your daughter to college). You should be happy." It's insulting, isn't it?

If we climb faster and faster up a ladder that's leaning against the wrong wall, we are really getting nowhere. We just keep going nowhere faster. And that's not really the point.

We have to focus on the right questions, the important factors in our lives.

It's Not Even About The Money

The important thing about money is not the money. It's never been about the money. It's always been about what the money can do.

If you had one trillion dollars in gold, silver and cash and were stranded on a desert island with no one around, no prospect of being found, no place to buy food, shelter or clothing, money would have absolutely no meaning. You'd have lots of money but no purchasing power. It's not about the money. It is about what it can be converted into. It's about the experiences it can create: what it can do for you and the people, institutions and causes you care most about.

It Is About: What's Important To YOU

I have yet to meet a successful professional who entered their profession just for the money. The money is a great by-product of what we do. But there's almost always a much deeper reason. It may be a sincere desire to help people, a love of science or the thrill of trying to solve a difficult problem (or a complex combination of these and many more).

My dad used to tell me, "Money doesn't buy happiness, but neither does poverty." Money can't buy happiness. Never has. Never will. Money can, however, pay for a safe place to live, vacation experiences that will last lifetimes or provide a sense of freedom to allow you to pursue your unique mission and passions. It can fund a college education, endow research to end a dreaded disease, feed starving children and provide a life of independence, free from the constraints of working just to get by.

One of the first steps in the process is defining what success really means to you. What's really important about money to you? Try this exercise: Get to a quiet, uninterrupted place for 10 minutes with a pen and a piece of paper and write down what's really important to you about money.

It's Like This

The Malted Milk Balls Disconnection

Before starting my own wealth management and financial planning firm, I worked as a stockbroker in downtown Nashville. Every day at 3:00 p.m. after the market close, I would walk down to the Peanut Shop in the "Arcade". They have the best malted milk balls on the planet. I would buy their smallest bag, 1/4 pound, of malted milk balls and eat them as I walked around, watched people and decompressed from the trading day. It was a comforting ritual. However, I also valued staying fit. After three years of my malted milk ball ritual every workday, I had gained 35 pounds. There was a disconnection between my value of staying fit and my behavior of eating malted milk balls. There is a financial disconnection going on today.

Several surveys of pre-retirees find that between 40% and 60% of them haven't done any retirement income planning.

Hope Is Not A Strategy

If you don't have enough money, there's not any product, strategy or cure other than continuing to work. But even for people who have accumulated enough money, what they're doing with their money and their expectations for their money often don't match.

The Retirement Confidence Survey, conducted by the Employee Benefits Research Institute, found that 24% thought they would live well in retirement and 26% believed they would have enough money to cover their basic needs. Only 23% thought they would <u>not</u> outlive their money. Look at that another way: 77% thought that they would outlive their money but most of them were still optimistic that they would have enough to live well or at least to cover basic needs. Being optimistic is great. It's important. It is basic to the American psyche. But we have to connect optimism with reality. Of those same people surveyed, 29% of the 55 and older crowd and 30% of the 45 to 54 group had saved less than $25,000.

It may be optimistic, but it's certainly not realistic, to think that $500,000 saved should be able to always produce a $60,000-a-year lifetime income. And all you need to do is find some great investment in a magazine on the newsstand or from this week's expert on a TV talk show and make 12%. There is a disconnection between expectations and reality.

Figuring Out the Combination

My son loves to pretend he's talking on the phone. When my parents call and I hold the phone up to my young son's ear, he'll listen for a moment and then back away and look suspiciously at the phone. He loves to play with the phone and pretend he's using it. But when he dials numbers, he's just randomly punching. He is too young to know how to answer the phone or use a phone book.

We have to make sure we don't plan for retirement income the same way. We could randomly dial numbers, hoping we come up with the right combination without ever consulting a phone book. That's like jumping from one investment to another, hoping by chance to find the jackpot. Or we could wait to use the phone until we're sure we know everything about the phone - how the signal knows to hop off at exactly the right house to reach the person

✓	RETIREMENT REALITY CHECK	↖

Realistic Expectations

For most people, financial goals fall into these broad categories:
- Enjoying a worry-free retirement without compromising your lifestyle.
- Contributing during or after your life to the financial security of your children or grandchildren.
- Creating a significant legacy to a beloved school, religious organization or charity.
- Providing quality long-term care for aging family members in a way that respects them and allows them to maintain their dignity.

we're trying to reach - instead of simply harnessing it's power and using it as a powerful tool.

When it comes to dialing the right phone number, hope is not a good strategy. You need to know the right combination of numbers to reach the person you want to call. Let's work toward putting success on your speed dial.

Focusing On Income

There are several major differences between the accumulation phase and the income (or "distribution" or "draw-down") phase. Young savers and investors can measure their progress using a benchmark for progress. For example: "I want to have a portfolio of $5,000,000 by January 1, 2010." There is a clear finish line and progress can be measured literally every day. During accumulation you can aim at a steady, predictable and controllable date. Reach the asset goal early? You have the option to retire early. Need to, or want to, work longer? Usually not a problem.

But when you get to the income phase you don't have the same tangible mark. You never know how long you (or your spouse) will live. Because of this, you can't forecast with much certainty how long your financial resources need to last. Income phase investment returns are used to meet real – and current – expenses. Since returns, whether on the stock market or on "fixed income" instruments like CDs, fluctuate substantially and unpredictably each year, creating a steady income stream is difficult.

Some of the risks with an income portfolio are much more complex than the types of financial hazards faced during the accumulation process. And the disturbing part for many folks is the realization that mistakes made in managing post-retirement risks are more difficult, even impossible, to correct or recover from. Yet all of these risks can be met and potentially and feasibly overcome - provided we understand the risks, and plan for them by creating a sound lifetime income plan.

SUMMING IT UP

o Demographic, economic, governmental and business trends will make it difficult for Baby Boomers to enjoy the kind of retirement they want – and expected.

o Success in retirement requires a focus on and understanding the income stage of your investment life.

o Many Boomers spend a lot of time and energy trying to find answers to the wrong questions when it comes to retirement planning.

1- Pension Benefit Guarantee Corporation
2- American Association of Retired Persons (AARP)

Chapter 2
THE GEORGE BURNS SYNDROME

Underestimating How Long You'll Live In 'Retirement'

"If I had known I'd live this long I would've taken better care of myself."
— George Burns

Where's The Grecian Formula?

There is a tremendous change going on in America that will have deep reaching implications for decades (that's plural) to come. America is getting older. Just look in the mirror. And while the biggest generation in our history is reaching retirement age, it's not just the Baby Boomers. The number of people over the age of 65 has increased from just 3 million a hundred years ago to more than 35 million in the year 2000. That number is expected to double to more than 70 million people over the next three decades and according to some estimates the number of people over the age of 85 is expected to increase over 225% during the next decade. Imagine more than three times as many people over age 85 in just the next 10 years! In fact, the "85 and over" crowd is the fastest growing segment of the United States population.

Of the success stories of the 20th Century, the sheer extension of the human life span is the one that seems most outstanding. Consider that at the founding of this country in 1776 the life expectancy at birth was just 23 years. In 1870 just 2.5% of the US population made it to age 65[1]. It is estimated that two thirds of all the people that have ever make it to age 65 are alive today. And 90% of the people who have lived to age 90 or beyond are alive today.

Advances in science and medical research have driven this success by increasing the likelihood that more infants live into adulthood and more 60-year-olds will live well into their 80s and 90s. New drugs, treatments, advancements in surgical procedures as well as the mapping of the human genome will make our lives and the lives of those we love better, longer and better longer. This increase in the over 65 population has frequently been termed "the graying of America."

Mick Jagger of the Rolling Stones was still bouncing around on-stage during his 2005 tour at the age of 62. Keith Richards is the same age. Performer Lena Horne, born in 1917, was still touring at the age of 85. She performed on television in 1997 for her 80th birthday celebration. Bob Hope was active almost into triple digits.

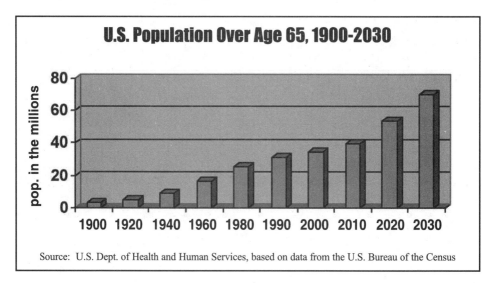

In 2001 my wife and I went to Kona, Hawaii to compete in the Half Ironman Triathlon. After the finish I felt a tremendous sense of accomplishment and sat and reflected on our 5 1/2-hour workout that day. Shortly after I finished I found myself on my feet, applauding along with a couple hundred other people for a 77-year-old Southern California man as he crossed the finish line. Seventy-seven years old. Our definition of "old" is changing. People are living longer than ever and the largest generation in our history is starting to retire. And they all need income.

WE'RE LIVING LONGER								
Life Expectancy in the U.S.								
Year	1930	1940	1950	1960	1970	1980	1990	2000	2001
Life Expectancy	59.7	62.9	68.2	69.7	70.8	73.7	75.4	76.9	77.2

Source: National Center for Health Statistics, National Vital Statistics Report, Vol. 51, No. 5, 03/03

In 1900 the life expectancy at birth was just 46 years old[2]. That number has steadily grown for a century in this country. For comparison, the average life expectancy at birth in Afghanistan today is still 46 years old. When social security was instituted in 1935, the average life expectancy in the US was under 60. What a great program! We'll start a retirement safety net that starts after most people aren't around anymore!

By 2002 there were almost five times as many people "working in retirement" than there were in total population over the age of 65 just 80 years earlier.

Don't Bet on Life Expectancy

When it comes to retirement income planning, life expectancy figures can be

It's Like This

THE AMAZING JEANNE CALMENT

Have you heard of Jeanne Calment? She was born in 1875 just outside of Paris, France. As a young woman Jeanne worked in her father-in-law's art supply business and sold canvas to Vincent Van Gogh. Now there's not anything remarkable about that; there were a lot of girls born just outside Paris in 1875 and there were a number of people in the art supply business. What is remarkable is that Jeanne lived until 1997. If you're quick at math, you've already figured out that Jeanne lived to be 122 years old. That's how Jeanne got into the Guinness Book of World Records for living the longest life that can be documented in modern times.

While Jeanne's story is somewhat amazing, all we have to do is look around us to see that people are living longer – much longer – than they did a generation or two ago. And not only are they living longer but they are much more active much longer.

What kind of retirement income plan did Jeanne need?

severely misleading. Many people will outlive their own "life expectancies."
This means that most people ought to think long and hard about "longevity risk" – the very real possibility of living 20, 30 or 40 years (or more)
past retirement age.

Averages can be deceiving. In fact, when you think about your own life
expectancy, it's probably much better to think about probabilities than averages.
While a healthy 65-year-old man has a life expectancy of age 81, he has a
50% probability of reaching age 85 and a 25% probability of reaching age 92.
For a woman age 65, the odds rise to a 50% chance of reaching 88 and a one-
in-four chance of living past her 94th birthday. The odds of at least one
member of a 65-year-old couple reaching 92 are 50%, and at least a 25%
chance of reaching 97[3].

RISK OF LIVING A LONG LIFE		
	50% Chance	**25% Chance**
Male Age 65	85	92
Female Age 65	88	94
Couple Age 65	92	97

Source: Society of Actuaries, Annuity 2000 Mortality Table. Figures assume a person is in good health.

The Longer You Live, The Longer You're Likely To Live

The longer you live, the longer you're likely to live. I know that sounds
idiotic at first, but here's what I mean. Life expectancies are based on averages
at birth. Since some people don't live until age 20, that brings the average
down. The fact that you've made it this far, bodes well for you living beyond

✓	RETIREMENT REALITY CHECK	↖

Realistic Expectations
Without proper planning, living a life longer than expected could easily allow
a person to outlive their money. This is probably the least understood variable
and risk in lifetime income planning. Few people have a clear sense of the
distinction between the life expectancy of their age group and the probability
that they will live years beyond their life expectancy.

your life expectancy at birth. If you reached age 60 today, your life expectancy is more than 81 years. If you reached age 80 today, your life expectancy is almost 90 years old.

There has never been a generation alive in history that has been faced with the challenge of the magnitude and scope that faces you today. Your retirement may last as long as your working life. What happens if you *DO* live to be 95, 100 or beyond? If you retire at 60, you may need income for another 35, 40 or 50 years. Will your income last as long as you do?

WE'RE LIVING LONGER IN RETIREMENT Life Expectancy when you reach age:								
Attained Age	20	30	40	50	60	70	80	90
Life Expectancy	78.1	78.6	79.2	80.2	81.2	84.6	88.8	94.8

Source: National Center for Health Statistics, National Vital Statistics Report, Vol. 51, No. 3, 12/02

Have You Planned for a 40-Year+ Retirement?

If you retire today at age 55, the reality is you may spend more time retired than you did working! If you planned enough retirement income to last to age 80 and you live to age 85, you have a 5-year "longevity gap."

The key is making certain your income lasts at least as long as you do! For previous generations this may have come in the traditional form. See if this sounds familiar: During the accumulation years, invest your retirement plans and other accounts into all equities. When you reach retirement, shift to bonds or fixed income investments for the steady income.

If we could rely on fixed income investments to keep up with inflation, that would be fine. But historically, they haven't. If, like previous generations, we were planning on a 10-year retirement, then there was no problem because you could spend some of your principal. But what if retirement lasts longer than you expected? There's the longevity gap and we have to have a strategy to at least keep up with the rising costs of living.

SUMMING IT UP

o People are living longer than ever before in history and there is a very real probability that Baby Boomers will outlive the standard life expectancy.

o A Boomers' retirement could last as long as their working life.

o Unless you are prepared, you could outlive your money.

o And you must have a strategy to keep up with the rising cost of living.

1- The Truth About Money by Rick Edelman
2- The Next Great Bubble Boom, Harry Dent
3 - Society of Actuaries, Annuity 2000 Mortality Table

Chapter 3
THE POSTAGE STAMP SYNDROME

Ignoring the Impact of Inflation

Did you see the movie *Austin Powers*? Austin was a secret agent who was cryogenically frozen in time back in the 1960s and brought back to life in the 1990s. His nemesis, Dr. Evil, who has also been frozen for 30 years, has plans to take over the world unless he collects

a ransom. With dramatic affect in his voice Dr. Evil first asks for a ransom of 'one m-i-l-l-i-o-n dollars.' The World Security Council erupts in laughter.

A million dollars isn't what it used to be. Cliché? Yes. True? Yes. "Inflation," as Sen. Alan Cranston has been quoted as saying, "isn't all bad. It has allowed every American to live in a more expensive neighborhood without moving."

The rising cost of goods and services is a very insidious risk. It's easy to ignore on a day-to-day basis. With inflation we lose by inches, not the cataclysmic stock market drops we see splashed in headlines. There is no alarm bell. We don't notice much change in our lifestyle when milk goes up $.05 a gallon or when gas goes up $.10 a gallon. If we do notice it, we soon forget.

Inflation impacts retirement income planning in two ways. First, it increases the future costs of goods and services. Second, it erodes the value of assets you have set aside to meet those costs.

In 1945 you could buy a new Chevy coupe for around

It's Like This

GOING POSTAL

In 1945 you could send three pieces of mail for a nickel: a first class letter and two postcards. That would run about $.83 today. When the stamp displayed above was issued in 1974, you could use it to send a first-class letter. Now it takes almost four of these. Soon, four of them won't do the trick. And it keeps going up, noticed about as much as a soft breeze.

$600. If you're not 65 or older, ask those who are how much they paid for their first home. Then ask them how much their current car cost when it was new. My bet is that the car they're driving now cost more than their first home.

During the last 10 or 15 years we have experienced what felt like a period of fairly low inflation. But in fact, in the 1990s, a low inflation decade by most recent standards, overall costs as measured by the Consumer Price Index rose by more than 30%. Over the course of the 20th century as a

A LOOK BACKWARD			
	1969	**1989**	**2005**
Bread	$.29	$1.29	$3.00
Tomato Soup	9 for $1.00	2 / $1.00	$1.50 ea.
Eggs	$.47	$1.19	$3.00

Source: U.S. Bureau of Labor Statistics

A LOOK BACKWARD AND FORWARD			
	1972	**2003**	**2033**
Stamp	$.10	$.37	$1.36?
Athletic Shoes	$9.00	$100	$1,000?
Candy Bar	$.10	$.89	$7.90?
New Car	$3,000	$23,000	$170,000?

Source: U.S. Bureau of Labor Statistics

✓ RETIREMENT REALITY CHECK 🔨

Realistic Expectations
Ask the question, "What is your greatest risk in retirement?" and most people will say "losing money." They're right. It's just that most people think of market losses. I would submit that inflation might be a much greater risk to your financial security throughout your entire investing life than market volatility. Inflation creeps in slowly causing insidious losses.

whole, inflation eroded ordinary Americans' purchasing power by about 95%. It takes $1 today buy what a nickel did in 1900.

Inflation is more the norm than the exception. The likelihood of inflation over the rest of your lifetime makes it imperative to beat inflation – especially during longer retirements.

Assume you wanted to retire with $120,000 of income. At just a 4% hypo-thetical inflation rate, in 10 years you would need $142,331 to buy the same stuff you bought at today's prices. In 20 years, you'd need $210,685, almost double, and that's at just 4%.

Now it may be easy to say you'd cut back as you

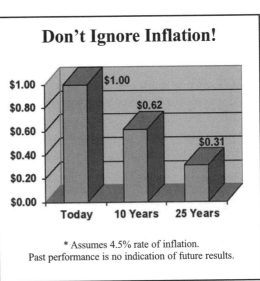

Don't Ignore Inflation!

* Assumes 4.5% rate of inflation.
Past performance is no indication of future results.

get older, but consider this: The prices of the 50 most commonly-used prescription drugs by the elderly rose on average of nearly twice the inflation rate between 1994 and 1999 - at a rate of 25.2% compared to 12.8% overall inflation over the same period[1]. In the year 2001, we continued to see a similar trend[2].

Our experience has been that there are two stages of retirement: the active stage and the healthcare stage. With advances in medicine the active stage can last longer. But the healthcare stage, while shorter, may be very expensive. In fact, of all the money Americans spend on healthcare in their lifetimes, about 80% of those dollars are spent in the last two years of life.

✓ RETIREMENT REALITY CHECK ⬈

What Is $273,750?
That is the Jeopardy question. The answer is: What amount could a couple spend on food during a 25 year retirement if you assume *NO* inflation, they eat three meals a day, seven days a week, at $5 per meal?

To continue to live in dignity and maintain quality of life, we need to make certain we're prepared for inflation in both stages.

If we stuff our money under the mattress we know we'll be going backwards, losing ground with each passing year. It is our responsibility as good stewards of our money to make certain our currency maintains its purchasing power.

We can't glance over this concept. Try to imagine this. Think of the car you're driving today, if you wanted to replace it with the equivalent in 25 years, if inflation continues about like it has over the last 25 years, then multiply the price of that automobile by three. In other words, if you're driving a $40,000 car, imagine that car costing $120,000. It's difficult to imagine, isn't it? We can't stick our heads in the sand on this topic. We have to consider the possibilities if we want to live a worry-free retirement.

Inflation Doesn't Stop Just Because You Retire!	
Year	**Annual Income Need**
1	$100,000
2	$104,000
3	$108,160
4	$112,486
5	$116,986
10	$142,331
15	$173,168
20	$210,685
25	$256,330
30	$311,865

Example illustrates annual income need of $100,000 increasing annually by an inflation rate of 4%.

My grandparents lived in Miami, Florida. When I was a kid I always thought of them as rich. They lived in a nice house, traveled the world, had been retired for years and traded for a brand new car every two years. Because of their experience with the Great Depression, my grandmother used to tell me that whatever I did, don't ever put any money in the stock market. She didn't.

As they got older their lifestyle seemed to be scaled back. So much so that by the time my grandmother and grandfather needed nursing care, they no longer seemed as rich. And they had rather limited choices in their later years. Their investments had preserved principal but hadn't preserved purchasing power.

Suppose you retired in 1975 with $1,000,000 and invested in interest bearing investments and spent only the interest. You may have been able to get 9%, generating $90,000 of income. The postage stamp was ten cents. What did a new car cost? Now fast forward 30 years to 2005. Your income has been cut by more than half. You didn't lose any principal, but your income is now $40,000. And the cost of a new car has tripled. The postage stamp has quadrupled. We need to adjust our thinking so we can conceptualize the need for an income that will double or triple during retirement.

We need to make certain we own investments that can help us stay ahead of the postage stamp risk. And certainly stocks may be one way to do that.

SUMMING IT UP

o Inflation is perhaps the greatest risk to the Baby Boomer's retirement – yet it is the most overlooked.

o Inflation is a double whammy for your retirement: while it increases the cost of goods and services, it simultaneously decreases the purchasing power of your investments.

o Cutting back on your lifestyle in retirement to account for inflation may not be an option – given that the most vital retirement expense, medication, increases faster than inflation.

o Our investments must be designed to stay ahead of inflation – especially given Boomers' longer life expectancy.

---

1 - Families, USA
2- CNN.com report: Drug costs for elderly continue to rise, June 12, 2001

Chapter 4

DISINHERITING YOUR UNCLE SAM

It's not what you make; it's what you keep that counts

Of the factors that will have an impact on your retirement income, what we've looked at so far are beyond your control. Most of us would consider living a longer life and being healthier than previous generations a good thing. A rising cost of living is something that we just have to deal with in our world. Those are realities we must adapt to, but they are out of your control. From here on out we're going to focus on factors where your behavior has a tremendous impact on the results.

One Dollar Doubled 21 Times is More than One Million Dollars

If you take one dollar and double it 21 times the total is more than one million dollars ($1x2=$2; $2x2=$4; $4x2=$8; etc.). But here's the really interesting part: If you tax the gain at just 31% each time you double that dollar, you won't end up with $1 million. In fact, you won't end up with even $600,000. Surely it's at least $100,000 right? Nope, when the return is eroded by taxes, you end up with just over $36,000!

| ✓ | RETIREMENT REALITY CHECK | 🔨 |

Realistic Expectations

What forces represent the biggest risk to your money? 1) Your Uncle (Sam) has a plan to spend your money both while you're alive and after you're gone. 2) The market and inflation can wreak havoc on your investments. 3) And a catastrophic health care event could leave you wiped out.

There is no investment exempt from all three risks. The good news is you can do something about each of these to eliminate or at least minimize their impact on you, your money and ultimately your life.

You see, the power of compounding is that powerful and the cost of taxes is that harmful to wealth creation. Albert Einstein is quoted as having said that compound interest is one of the wonders of the modern world. Taxation erodes the compounding effect on money.

Now let me be perfectly clear: I think everyone should pay taxes. I mean everyone. It's part of living in the wonderful country we call the United States. Taxes do some great things for us: provide interstates, protection, police forces and National Parks. I believe we should each pay our fair share and not a penny more. But remember, it's not what you make, it's what you keep that counts.

Taxes

Let's face it; taxes are your biggest expense. Taxes are bigger than your mortgage payment (if you still have one), bigger than your kids or grandkids' college expenses. If you own a business, you pay FICA, FUTA, SUTA, Social Security, Federal, State and Local and property taxes. In Tennessee, we also get to pay a "professional privilege tax," as well as a hefty sales tax.

It's Like This

ALL THAT JAZZ

Jazz, like any other music, has certain rules. You start with a framework called the song. It has a melody and a basic harmonic content around the melody. But one song can be played a number of ways with different rhythms, styles and chord substitutions.

With jazz you hear certain motifs or riffs. Often these are rhythmic motifs that are repeated with variations of pitch. If you learn to play a lot of music in one genre you begin to notice certain patterns emerge repeatedly.

Music and money have a lot in common. They are both very personal. What works for one person doesn't work the same way for another. There are certain patterns present in each. Charts may be used in each discipline to make visual sense of the concepts and to communicate those concepts.

If you think about it, dealing with your money is a lot like making music. There are certain principals, rules if you will, to follow. And you begin to notice patterns that repeat, in music, in the economy and in markets.

Taxes reduce our ability to meet our objectives and many off-the-shelf, one-size fits all solutions don't adequately work. We should never fall victim to making decisions based solely only on a hatred of paying taxes without considering if the investment makes good economic sense. However, we still have to take the cost of taxes into account. Taxes are a huge added expense.

Tax Diversification or Asset "Location"

Diversification, often called "asset allocation" is something the investment community loves to talk about. We seem enamored with pretty colored pie charts. But TRUE diversification includes not only asset allocation, or asset diversification, but also TAX Diversification. We call it "asset location" because the type of account you use to hold your money frequently determines its tax status.

Our choices for tax diversification are limited by the definitions of the Internal Revenue Code and they are:

1) Taxable or
2) Tax-Deferred or
3) Tax-Free

☞ CAN YOU IMAGINE: ☜
Losing Coming and Going

Bill had recently retired when he and Harriet went to see an advisor in 2002. Having been a contract engineer and having spent several years overseas, Bill had made investments and done his taxes himself without much help. After all, he was an engineer with more than average intelligence.

Bill and Harriet needed about $7,000 per month to live the lifestyle they wanted. As the advisor reviewed their two previous years' tax returns he saw that their investment income had been over $160,000. Here's where it gets interesting. Although their "income" had been over $160,000 for the previous two years, their investments had actually lost money – to the tune of about $450,000. The insult added to injury was the $90,000 of taxes they paid on investments that had lost value.

Bill and Harriet hadn't overpaid their taxes; they simply failed to structure their investments in a tax-efficient manner. Even though the stock market took their investments down in value, the 1099 tax forms kept coming.

The Federal Government's General Accounting Office reports that more than 2 million Americans are overpaying their taxes to the tune of about $945,000,000 – almost $1 Billion – per year because of missed credits and deductions they are entitled to. But that doesn't even start to take into account credits and deductions that weren't missed because people didn't properly plan to get them in the first place. Bill and Harriet's taxes weren't counted in the GAO's report. They simply failed to do smart tax planning. No one had helped them understand the impact of the types of investments they held.

Bill and Harriet are smart people. But the current version of the Federal Tax Code is 17,000 pages long. The IRS doesn't give a tax break for being smart to people who don't take proper action.

Taxable Investments

When I first got started in this business, I had the hardest time understanding why some people seemed to focus almost exclusively on their hatred of paying taxes. I want to pay my fair share, but not a dime more. And then I had my first 'opportunity' to pay more in tax than I had earned in an entire year just a few short years before. That was when I had my personal tax wake-up call.

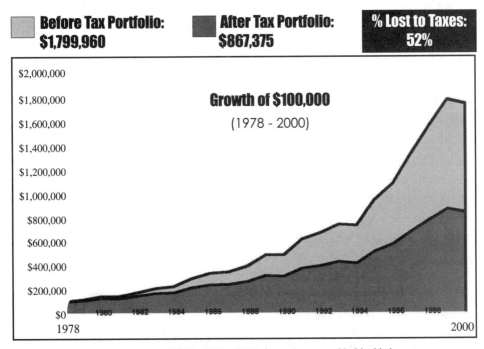

| Before Tax Portfolio: $1,799,960 | After Tax Portfolio: $867,375 | % Lost to Taxes: 52% |

Growth of $100,000
(1978 - 2000)

Source: SEI: 60% Wilshire 5000, 40% Lehman Aggregate, No Liquidation
Interest income and dividends are taxed annually at historical top marginal tax rates; capital gains are realized at 50% per year and are taxed at the historical long-term capital gains tax rate.
Past performance is no guarantee of future results.

In the graph you can easily see that it's not just a little bit of money that's being lost to your Uncle in a tax-inefficient portfolio, it's also the future earnings or compounding on those dollars. This graph assumes that *only* half of the capital gains are realized and are simply taxed at the then current tax rates. Imagine how much would be lost to taxes if more of the capital gain were realized each year! Taxes have a significant impact.

What can you do to make your taxable assets more tax-efficient? One thing is to use investment vehicles that, when they do generate gains, generate only (or mostly) long-term gains. Another option is to implement active tax-management strategies to enhance after-tax returns.

"Loss harvesting" is one active tax-management strategy that can be implemented to realize losses to offset gains. For example, you might sell a stock just as it goes ex-dividend thereby realizing a loss equal to the approximate value of the dividend. Dollar-wise, it's about a wash but a loss for tax purposes is generated. For most individuals it may not be very effective to try to do it on your own because of the costs involved, but it is an example of what is possible.

Do you know how much future income you're giving up because of tax inefficiency?

Little Things Mean A Lot

Many people don't take advantage of the resources available to help them save on taxes. A little bit here and there doesn't seem to make a difference. It may seem irrelevant or so small it's imperceptible.

Here is why I am so passionate about helping people in this area: Instead of thinking "what could have been" - what if you were able to arrange your affairs or the way you take your income distributions so they were just

---

✓   RETIREMENT REALITY CHECK   ⟍

Decisive Action

Don't make the mistake so many people make of waiting until April 15 to do any tax planning (when it is too late, of course). Hopefully, you have a good CPA. If you don't, you should find one and schedule a brief consultation with him or her before year-end each year to ensure you don't have negative surprises come April 15.

You deserve an accountant who is more than just a historian. Historians deal with what happened in the past. They tell you what happened and how much you owe as a result. The great accountants help you with tax planning and help you minimize taxes. Be careful about getting your tax advice and your investment planning advice from the same person. Both disciplines are full-time professions. It's difficult for one person to truly be a professional at both.

$2,000 more tax efficient each year – what if you simply took this money and instead of giving it to your Uncle Sam you placed it in a Roth IRA for your child, grandchild, nephew, or a friend's child? (Assuming they had at least $2,000 of earned income per IRS Publication 590). Or you could even keep the money for yourself! And suppose you were to do this for the next seven years… What an amazing impact you could have on the future. (Withdrawals at retirement from a Roth IRA are income tax-free).

☞ CAN YOU IMAGINE: ✍

When A Loss Is A Gain

John started his own business after leaving a company as chief financial officer. John understands numbers. So when he got a statement showing a realized loss of $65,000 on an investment he recently made, he was upset. Upon closer examination and after talking with his advisor, he realized his investment was actually worth about $200,000 more than he had invested. Because of the tax structure of the strategy he was using, it had generated a "realized loss" (that's a loss as far as the IRS is concerned) although the investment had actually gone up in value. That realized loss was used to offset taxes on his less tax-efficient investments.

Eventually the whole thing was cashed in, he realized the gains for tax purposes and he paid taxes at the low long-term gains rate.

✓　RETIREMENT REALITY CHECK　🔨

Knowledge

Since long-term capital gains are currently taxed at the 15% bracket and short-term gains are taxed at ordinary income brackets which may be in excess of 30%, it certainly makes sense to be able to control your buy and sell decisions. Many investments do let you decide when you'll pay taxes. Many investments don't! Just because you're a long-term investor doesn't mean your investments are taxed like nothing was ever sold. You have to know about your particular situation.

For the long haul, consider that long-term capital gains and dividends are currently taxed at a maximum rate of 15%. Taxation on capital gains hasn't been this low since 1933 - 72 years ago. Dividends haven't been taxed at a lower rate since 1916 or 89 years ago. (Source: Forbes, Smith & Crouch CPAs)

THE POWER OF COMPOUNDING

Susie: Start investing at age 16			Lucky, Jr.: Investing at age 26		
Invest $2,000 per year for 8 years			**Invest $2,000 per year for 35 years**		
(Assuming a 10% Hypothetical Rate of Return and that Susie has at least $2,000 of earned income so a Roth could be utilized.)			(Assuming a 10% Hypothetical Rate of Return and that Lucky has at least $2,000 of earned income so a Roth could be utilized.)		
Age	**Investments**	**Total Values**	**Age**	**Investments**	**Total Value**
16	$2,000	$2,200	16	$0	$0
17	$2,000	$4,620	17	$0	$0
18	$2,000	$7,282	18	$0	$0
19	$2,000	$10,210	19	$0	$0
20	$2,000	$13,431	20	$0	$0
21	$2,000	$16,974	21	$0	$0
22	$2,000	$20,871	22	$0	$0
23	$2,000	$25,159	23	$0	$0
24	$0	$29,875	24	$0	$0
25	$0	$35,062	25	$0	$0
26	$0	$38,568	26	$2,000	$2,200
27	$0	$42,425	27	$2,000	$4,620
8	$0	$46,668	28	$2,000	$7,282
29	$0	$51,334	29	$2,000	$10,210
30	$0	$56,468	30	$2,000	$13,431
31	$0	$62,115	31	$2,000	$16,974
32	$0	$68,326	32	$2,000	$20,871
33	$0	$75,159	33	$2,000	$25,159
34	$0	$82,675	34	$2,000	$29,875
35	$0	$90,942	35	$2,000	$35,062
36	$0	$100,037	36	$2,000	$40,769
37	$0	$110,040	37	$2,000	$47,045
38	$0	$121,044	38	$2,000	$53,950

SUSIE			LUCKY, JR.		
Age	Investments	Total Values	Age	Investments	Total Value
39	$0	$133,149	39	$2,000	$61,545
40	$0	$146,464	40	$2,000	$69,899
41	$0	$161,110	41	$2,000	$79,089
42	$0	$177,221	42	$2,000	$89,198
43	$0	$194,944	43	$2,000	$100,318
44	$0	$214,438	44	$2,000	$112,550
45	$0	$235,882	45	$2,000	$126,005
46	$0	$259,470	46	$2,000	$140,805
47	$0	$285,417	47	$2,000	$157,086
48	$0	$313,959	48	$2,000	$174,995
49	$0	$345,355	49	$2,000	$194,694
50	$0	$379,890	50	$2,000	$216,364
51	$0	$417,879	51	$2,000	$240,200
52	$0	$459,667	52	$2,000	$266,420
53	$0	$505,633	53	$2,000	$295,262
54	$0	$556,197	54	$2,000	$326,988
55	$0	$611,817	55	$2,000	$361,887
56	$0	$672,998	56	$2,000	$400,276
57	$0	$740,298	57	$2,000	$442,503
58	$0	$814,328	58	$2,000	$488,953
59	$0	$895,761	59	$2,000	$540,049
60	$0	$985,337	60	$2,000	$596,254
Total Amount Invested = $16,000 **Ending Value = $985,337**			**Total Amount Invested = $70,000** **Ending Value = $596,254**		

This is a hypothetical example and it is not intended to imply the performance of any specific investment.
Your own investment experience may be better or worse than this example.

Little things can mean a lot! Especially with the power of compounding.

Tax-Deferred

Tax-deferred investments provide the opportunity for growth of investment, growth of the reinvested gains and growth of the amounts that you don't pay in taxes. Tax-deferral allows for your money to grow free of taxation until you get ready to spend it.

There is a widespread idea that goes like this: "If I'm already in a high tax bracket, I might as well go ahead and pay taxes now, because my tax rate may go higher in the future because tax rates may go up and I'm likely to have the same income in retirement that I do now." Income tax rates very well may go up over the next 30 years. This may sound like it makes sense on the surface, but let's dig deeper.

You may have heard of the "Rule of 72." The rule is a simple calculation that demonstrates how long it will take your investment to double at a particular rate of return. The formula is this:

72 ÷ growth rate = estimated number of years to double investment*

So if you earn 7.2% each year on an investment, it will take about 10 years for the investment to double (72 / 7.2 = 10). If you earned 6% each year on an investment it would take about 12 years for the investment to double (72 / 6 = 12). At 12% it will take an investment about 6 years to double in value. It's a good rule of thumb to use to make it easy to do compound interest calculations.

Now, let's use the Rule of 72 to determine the potential advantage (or disadvantage) of tax-deferred investing.

Let's look at an example using a 9% hypothetical rate of return and a 33% combined tax rate. Bob and Sue both invested money for growth. Bob invested in a taxable account and Sue invested in a tax-deferred account. Bob earns 9% on his taxable investments and since he's in a 33% tax bracket, he nets about a 6% after tax return. Sue is in the same tax bracket and earns the same 9% but she has opted to invest in a tax-deferred investment account.

TAXABLE illustration (Bob)	TAX-DEFERRED illustration (Sue)
$100,000 starting investment	$100,000 starting investment
9% rate of return	9% rate of return
33% tax rate	33% tax rate
33% tax rate on 9% = 6% net rate	0% tax rate on 9% = 9% net rate
12 years to double investment value	8 years to double investment value
72 / 6 = 12 years	72 / 9 = 8 years
Start: $100,000	Start: $100,000
12 years: $200,000	8 years: $200,000
24 years: $400,000	16 years: $400,000
	24 years: $800,000
After tax value = $400,000	**After tax value = $569,000** (assuming lump sum) = $700,000 x 33% = $231,000 in taxes owed; $800,000 -$231,000 = $569,000

Taxable illustration assumes no withdrawals and a 33% tax rate. Most tax-deferred accounts are subject to ordinary income tax rates upon withdrawal and if taken prior to age 59 1/2 may be subject to a federal income tax penalty. This is a hypothetical example and it is not intended to imply the performance of any specific investment. Your own investment may perform better or worse than this example. *The Rule of 72 is based on compounding a fixed rate of return over a long period of time. However, most investments generate fluctuating returns so the period of time in which an investment can double cannot be determined with certainty.

NOTE: Tax law is complex and subject to change (is that an understatement?). The author does not practice law or accounting in the state of Tennessee or any other state.

Bob's investment doubles in value every 12 years, so his $100,000 turns into $200,000 in 12 years. Over the next 12 years it doubles again from $200,000 to $400,000. Sue's investment doubles in 8 years because she doesn't have to pay taxes along the way on the earnings she makes each year. So in eight years she has $200,000. In the next eight she has $400,000 and by the time 24 years has rolled by she has $800,000. Sue has twice as much money as Bob.

Now, assume they both decide to cash the investments out to buy a second home. Bob will cash out $400,000 – he's already paid taxes on his growth. Sue will cash out $569,000 (she pays tax on the $700,000 profit she made). Sue gets 169% more money based on her initial investment than Bob. Sue nets about 42% MORE dollars than Bob.

☞ CAN YOU IMAGINE: ☜
Writing Uncle Sam Out Of The Will

Leonard and Joan have two major passions in their lives: their family and their church. Leonard has gone on mission trips to third world countries and Joan teaches classes and is involved in numerous out-reach programs through their church. They have two kids and three grandchildren they adore. Everything in their lives revolves around those two passions.

When Leonard and Joan sat down to do the basic estate planning session, their advisor mapped out what they wanted to have happen - while they were alive and after each passed on. No surprise that it came down to helping their kids and grandkids, their church and supporting missions. Fortunately, they were able to work together with their advisor to cut out one of their major heirs, Uncle Sam.

Uncle Sam already has an estate plan prepared for everyone. With some simple techniques Leonard and Joan were able to cut what would go to their Uncle to the tune of about $257,300. The key for them was that by retitling some assets and signing a few documents, they were able to increase what would go to their kids and their church by $257,300. It's certainly not all the money in the world, but like Leonard said, "a quarter of a million bucks is a quarter of a million bucks."

The epilogue to the story is that once the documents were finalized to put in place everything the couple wanted, it took almost five months before they stopped to sign what needed to be signed to get what they wanted - even though they drove past the attorney's office every day on their way into town.

With estate planning there is a real sense of having to face one's own mortality.

But what if they both wanted income from their investments? Don't most people at some point want income? In that scenario, the tax-deferred account would have an even greater advantage over the taxable funds. Using the same assumptions, let's assume they both continue to earn exactly 9% and take the earnings as income each year. Bob gets $36,000 of taxable income and Sue gets $72,000 of taxable income without touching principal. Sue gets twice as much income!

What If Tax Rates Go Up?

The standard "logic" given for not wanting to invest tax-deferred is "what happens if tax rates go up?" Let's look back to Bob and Sue.

Assume they both continue to make 9% but the day before they both start taking income, tax rates jump to 50%. Bob is feeling like he made a smart decision because he paid the taxes as he went. However, Bob will still get $36,000 per year taxed at 50% and Sue will get $72,000 per year taxed at 50%. Sue still gets twice as much income.

What if they decided to cash out to buy that vacation home, assuming an overnight tax increase to 50%? Bob would still have the $400,000 and Sue would have just $450,000. Not as much difference. (However, if tax rates had increased gradually over the 24-year period, there would be an even larger discrepancy between Bob and Sue in favor of Sue.)

Qualified Plans

One way you can reduce your current income taxes and make serious headway toward retirement is to maximize your contributions to your quali-fied plan(s). During the accumulation phase, you probably set aside all you knew you could before tax in order to make the most out of lowering your current taxes and having the benefit of allowing the money to accumulate without the taxation.

As of this writing there are more than 10 kinds of IRAs alone. That doesn't include 401(k) (pick your flavor: age-weighted, comparability tested, safe harbor, etc.), Money Purchase, 403(b), 457, 408, and on and on. And contribution limits are changing as well as catch-up provisions. Is it any wonder most people are a little confused?

And what is the maximum amount that can be contributed pre-tax — before one dime of tax is taken out? Is it $4,000? $10,000? $14,000?

$40,000? $100,000? $165,000? The answer may be "yes," but it depends on many factors in your specific situation. This is where knowing how to work the Rubik's Cube of financial planning comes in very helpful.

While making contributions to qualified plans is really a key component of the accumulation phase of investing, the focus here is on making the most of retirement income. So, we'll mention these in general terms for the purpose of overview. Make certain you speak with a qualified professional who can help you sort this out if you're still in the accumulation phase because maximizing your contributions to a qualified plan can have significant benefits, not only at retirement, but to each year's income as the tax savings are considered.

Defined Contribution

A defined contribution plan is one where the contribution amount or limit is the known amount. You know how much you can contribute to a 401(k), you just don't know what the benefit will be when you take the money out. Companies like defined contribution plans because the risk of investing is shifted from the employer

---

━◖ WHAT DAD SAID ◗━

My Dad's Favorite Poem

*A*long *with sociology, my dad taught English for many years. My dad is not the kind to talk a whole lot. Being a man of few words, he's certainly not the kind to go around quoting poetry very often. But I do remember several times going to him for one-on-one talks and asking for advice and he'd share lines from his favorite poem, Rudyard Kipling's "If".*

If you can keep your head when all about you
Are losing theirs and blaming it on you;
If you can trust yourself when all men doubt you,
But make allowance for their doubting too;
If you can wait and not be tired by waiting,
Or being lied about, don't deal in lies,
Or being hated, don't give way to hating,
And yet don't look too good, nor talk too wise;

If you can dream - and not make dreams your master;
If you can think - and not make thoughts your aim;...

If you can talk with crowds and keep your virtue,
Or walk with kings - nor lose the common touch,
If neither foes nor loving friends can hurt you,
If all men count with you, but none too much;
If you can fill the unforgiving minute
With sixty seconds' worth of distance run -
Yours is the Earth and everything that's in it,
And - which is more - you'll be a Man, my son!

to the employee. There is no promise about future income. If the employee doesn't contribute enough to fund a comfortable retirement, well, that's not the company's problem.

Contribution amounts are made with pre-tax dollars. Each individual decides how much to invest up to pre-set limits. That amount can grow in an account that is exempt from taxation until the money is withdrawn. Once withdrawn, the entire withdrawal is subject to income tax at the then current tax rate. Of course, withdrawals prior to age 59 may be subject to a federal tax penalty of 10%-25% in addition to income tax, depending on they type of plan.

Defined Benefit

Defined benefit plans are a rarer breed these days. They define what the benefit will be at retirement. These are usually called a pension. Defined benefit plans take the investment risk off of the individual and place it on the company.

Small companies or professionals with few (or no) employees often opt for this type of plan because so much more money can be put away – in some cases almost ten times as much as in a 401(k) – and sheltered from current taxation and taxation on the earnings until it is withdrawn at retirement.

Tax-Free

There are not many true tax shelters left. Income from state municipal bonds is still exempt from federal taxation. If you are in the top income tax brackets and are likely to remain there, you could derive some benefit from earning interest that is exempt from federal (and in some cases, state) taxation. However, if you are in a lower tax bracket, say the 25% bracket, the benefit from the tax-free income may be questionable.

If you are already collecting Social Security income, the income from municipal bonds is tax-exempt, but it *does* count in the calculation that may cause your Social Security income to be subject to taxation. Interest from municipal bonds may be subject to state and local taxes as well as the Alternative Minimum Tax (AMT). Additionally, the yields on these bonds may be somewhat low. But it is certainly one option.

Roth IRAs

A Roth IRA is simply a type of account that allows you to contribute after-tax money. The investments inside of the Roth grow tax-deferred and when you make withdrawals at retirement the money you get is income tax-free.

✍ CAN YOU IMAGINE: ✍

To Deduct or Not To Deduct?

Art called one day to apprise his advisor of a change in his personal situation. Because they had a good working relationship for more than a decade, Art called for advice before buying or leasing a car to double-check that he wasn't missing something.

Art's wife wanted to remodel the kitchen. They had gotten bids and planned on spending about $40,000 on the upgrade. Art had already filled the paperwork out and was ready to send it in for a line of credit against their home for the upgrade. The advisor asked why they didn't plan on using some of their cash that was sitting in money market, since they usually kept $100,000 to $200,000 liquid. Art said he figured since the loan was at such a low interest rate and since it was tax-deductible, it would make more sense to borrow it.

Now you may think that every financial planner would agree with that. And there are some good ones who might. Art said since the interest rate was low and it would be tax deductible, he thought it would make more sense to borrow than to spend his cash.

His advisor told him it wouldn't be deductible for him and, knowing his aversion to debt, recommended he just use the money from money market. Art called the advisor the next day with a confession. "After our conversation, what you told me was so counter intuitive I called my son-in-law who is an accountant and asked him. He said he'd figure it out on a spreadsheet or something. He called back and said, yeah, I think that's right. It doesn't look like you should borrow the money. It still sounded so opposite of what I thought to be true that I called my CPA. He told me the same thing. I just wanted to say 'thanks' for disagreeing with me. And I know you have a vested interest in us keeping more money with you instead of less."

If you qualify, you should contribute to a Roth IRA and consider converting your existing IRAs to a Roth. A word of caution: if you convert an existing IRA to a Roth you will have to pay income tax on the amount you convert so don't do a conversion without the assistance of a qualified professional.

In order to qualify for the maximum Roth IRA contribution, you must have earned income (not just investment income) and make less than $150,000 per year if you're married and filing joint tax returns or earn less than $90,000 if you're single. There is a lesser amount you can contribute if you earn over those figures, but you can't contribute at all if you earn over $160,000 for those married filing joint tax returns or $110,000 for single filers. The people who can benefit most from Roths don't qualify. And if you're older, the contribution limits won't allow you to accumulate a great deal of wealth anyway.

Wouldn't it make sense to be truly diversified? Doing so includes tax diversification. There may be other tax-free investments you qualify for depending on your specific situation. You'll want to get together with someone qualified in this area to determine what works best for you.

The bottom line is that to be truly diversified, you will want to have some money that is taxable, some that is tax-deferred and some that is tax-free.

Remember, it's not what you make, it's what you keep that counts.

It's Like This

I was riding my mountain bike on a trail in Chattanooga. There was one section going down the side of the mountain that cut between a big rock on the right and a big log on the left. But there was enough clearance for about two inches on either side of my tires. The first two times down were uneventful. The third time I approached the section, I looked at how big that log was and how steep the drop to the right was. Of course that time I hit the log and flew over the handlebars. I learned why you should always look where you want to go.

A few years later I was helping my daughter learn to ride a bike. I was running along side her on a flat, paved, easy path. She saw a pedestrian on the opposite side of the road, swerved hard right out of my reach, off the path and into a thicket of briars.

I picked her up, hugged her, pulled out a couple of thorns and asked her why she was crying so hard. She said, "I didn't look where I wanted to go. I looked where I didn't want to go."

Financially, there are always going to be things to distract us along the way. Having a clear plan helps us look where we want to go.

SUMMING IT UP

o   Taxes are Boomers' biggest expense, yet they represent one area of their financial lives that they have some control over - if they plan ahead.

o   Many Boomers overpay taxes.

o   Tax diversification is as important as asset allocation.

o   There are three choices for tax diversification: 1) Taxable, 2) Tax-Deferred and 3) Tax Free.

o   Even if you are in a high tax bracket and expect the same income during retirement, tax deferred investments can make sense.

o   See a professional to get your tax house in order. Tax law is too complicated for non-professionals to tackle with confidence.

Chapter 5
RISK AND RETURN

Understanding the Market

"It's not what we know that hurts us. It's what we know that isn't so."

Where are we so far? We now understand that we need to plan for a retirement that may last several times as long as our parents. During that retirement we need to allow for an income that will go up at least at the rate of an increasing cost of living. Taxes, or the appropriate reduction in taxes, can play a significant role in our ability to meet those challenges. Now let's look at broad categories of investments that can be used to meet those challenges.

In my opinion, the financial services industry has done a pretty good job of educating people when about the accumulation stage. However, there is a dearth of information on how the rules change during the income stage when risks that have little bearing during the accumulation phase become critical.

As we move through this section there will be a number of examples given. Please keep in mind that they are all hypothetical examples and are not a portrayal of past or future investment performance for any specific investment. Your own investment results may be better or worse than these examples and the examples do not include costs or taxes which could have a dramatic effect on results. And, of course, past performance is no guarantee of future results (which we'll talk more about later).

The Basics

First of all, when it comes right down to it, there are really only two options for our money. We can 'own' or we can 'loan.' If you have a Certificate of Deposit or a savings account, you're really loaning money to a company in exchange for interest payments. If you buy a piece of property or a fraction of a company (a stock), you own it. Own or loan.

Second, there is no such thing as a risk-free investment. There are, however different kinds of risk and it is important to understand what they are. Every investment is flawed. There is no 'perfect' investment; only investments that are flawed in ways that you can live with. Deciding on investments is like deciding on a spouse. You don't find a 'perfect' person although you may have found the perfect person for you. You look for someone with flaws that you can live with and with benefits you do not want to live without!

Third, you often hear investments referred to as investment vehicles. They are a lot like cars. There is no 'perfect' one but each will work much better if you match the vehicle with its intended use. You wouldn't pull a horse trailer with a Ferrari. You wouldn't think of driving to a New York business meeting in an F-350 dualie truck. (Can you imagine even trying to get that in a parking garage?) You wouldn't drive a NASCAR stock car on a family vacation. Each vehicle is designed with a specific purpose in mind. Use it for something radically different and, in the best situation, you won't get where you want to go; in the worst situation you'll wreck, hurting yourself and your family in the process.

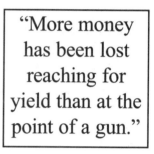

"More money has been lost reaching for yield than at the point of a gun."

How Do You Spell Risk?

Often in low interest rate environments people begin looking for a higher yield at the expense of safety. As Will Rogers said, "People should be more concerned with the return of their money than the return on their money."

✓　　**RETIREMENT REALITY CHECK**　　🔨

Realistic Expectations
"The first generation of 401(k) savers, which has already taken on unprecedented responsibility to manage their own retirement, now has to figure out how to make their funds last 25 to 30 years."
"A $1 million portfolio has a one-in-seven chance of leaving you broke within 30 years if you withdraw $40,000 in the first year and increase your payments with inflation." (Business Week Investor Guide, July 28, 2003)

It's important that we develop a broad understanding of risk. If I were to ask you: "How do you define risk?" or "What do you think is the biggest risk?" Most people would answer, "The risk of losing my principal." I think that's a great answer. But does it go deep enough?

Suppose you could invest in something that had never lost principal. Sounds safe so far, right? But the *real return* (the return after taxes and inflation) was negative 30% of the time. As far as past performance goes, its best one-year real rate of return in the last two decades was 2.18%. Sound like a good investment? You're going backwards one out of three years and the biggest up year in the last 20 was a paltry 2%. Would you call that a safe investment? A wise investment?

Certificates of Deposit have performed exactly in this manner, based on the average rates for 6-month CDs over a 20-year period. But they have never lost principal.[1]

What if you could invest in something that had not had a losing 20-year period over the past 100 years? Would that sound like a safe investment? It would as long as you could afford to leave the money set aside for 20 years. That's what the stock market has done. However, invest in the stock market and look 6-months later. Now does that look safe? Not a chance.

✐ CAN YOU IMAGINE: ✎
Emotion and Investment Decisions

Candice went to see a comprehensive planner because she had been working with a stockbroker and felt like she needed a more comprehensive review. Her main complaint was that she was not happy with the rate of return over the previous 15 years.

Almost 75% of her portfolio was made up of one stock inherited from her father. The return on the stock for 15 years was less than the average annual return for money market accounts over the same 15 years. When the planner mentioned that this one stock might be responsible for the lack of performance she was concerned about, he discovered an important factor. That stock wasn't just an investment, to Candice it represented her father and his love for her. How could she make a rational decision when there was this emotionally charged linkage between an investment and her deceased father? Candice agreed to diversify by selling most of the stock with the understanding that she would keep a few shares with the intention of never selling them. Also, getting one share of stock in certificate form and having it framed was also a nice reminder of how much her father loved her. And it allowed her to invest most of her money in a way that was more appropriate for her.

What I'd like to challenge you to do is to reevaluate and redefine your perspective on risk. Risk changes over time. The longer period of time we're dealing with, the more we have to be aware of risks other than day-to-day fluctuations in market value of investments.

Historical Real Rates of Return		
Year	**CD Rate**	**Return After Taxes & Inflation**
1981	15.50%	-3.92%
1982	12.18%	2.18%
1983	9.65%	1.00%
1984	10.65%	1.32%
1985	7.82%	.11%
1986	6.30%	2.03%
1987	6.58%	-.37%
1988	8.15%	1.39%
1989	8.27%	1.25%
1990	7.85%	-.43%
1991	4.95%	.34%
1992	3.27%	-.63%
1993	2.88%	-.98%
1994	5.40%	.58%
1995	5.21%	.59%
1996	5.21%	-.17%
1997	5.71%	1.72%
1998	5.34%	1.59%
1999	5.43%	.58%
2000	6.64%	.59%

Past performance is no guarantee of future performance. Taxes are federal only for highest rate as listed in the Advisory Commission on Intergovernmental Relationships/Significant Features of Fiscal Federalism. Bank certificates of deposit rates are calculated using six-month annualized average monthly CD rate reported by the Federal Reserve Board. Band CDs, which are insured by the FDIC for up to $100,000, are short-term investments that pay fixed principal and interest but are subject to fluctuating rollover rates and early withdrawal penalties. Inflation rates are based on the Consumer Price Index (CPI), a measure of change in consumer prices, as determined by the U.S. Bureau of Labor Statistics.

The R Word

One of the key principals of risk management is to make sure money placed in the equity markets has the time to do what equities are usually good at doing – keeping ahead of inflation. Money in the equity markets for short term needs is a bad idea. The one exception to this principle, in my opinion, is if you are in a position to you need only the dividends generated by equities. As of this writing, the dividend yield on the broad market is around 1.5%. If you need to generate only 1.5% cash flow from your portfolio to live a comfortable lifestyle, then congratulations. (Keep in mind, dividends are based on corporate profits and are not guaranteed.)

Stocks Big And Small

You probably already know that large company stocks or indexes that include them like the Dow Jones Industrial Average and the Standard & Poor's 500 index tend to have more consistent performance than small company stocks and their respective indices. And you know that small company stocks have delivered better results over long periods of time but have had much more fluctuation, including more negative years, than big company stocks. Over long periods, typically ten years or more, stocks fairly consistently trounce the performance of fixed income investments like bonds. But in short time frames, stocks can go down. A lot. The key is that you don't ever want to be forced to sell an asset in a compressed market.

Long Term Perspective

You've seen the charts and graphs which tell you that since 1926 stocks have averaged slightly over 10% and long-term government bonds have averaged a little over 5% before the effects of taxes and inflation.[2]

And I'm sure you know from reading or from your own experience that small company stocks tend to have much more fluctuation than large company stocks and they have more fluctuation than most bonds. And over the long haul, it has been much more profitable to be an <u>owner</u> of great businesses than to be a <u>loaner</u> to great businesses.

You may come to the conclusion at this point that what I am advocating is that everyone should always be invested in the stock market. But you haven't yet heard the entire story.

The Truth About Returns: Gains and Losses Are Not Created Equal

Losses hurt. Not only is the subjective emotional pain excruciating, but the objective financial losses are difficult to recover from. Let me illustrate. Suppose you had an investment that lost 10% one year and made 10% the next. You started with $100,000 and lost 10% you now have $90,000. If you make 10% you will then have $99,000. That's 1% less than you started with. You're not even. Down 10% and up 10% leaves you with a loss.

The larger the loss is, the greater the subsequent recovery would have to be to break even. For example, we know that a 30% loss takes a 43% gain to break even and a 40% loss takes a 67% gain to break even. Even a 20% loss takes a 25% gain to get back to even.

Let's look at this from another perspective. From its peak on March 10, 2000 to its low point of October 9, 2002 (the low point as of this writing), The NASDAQ Composite index dropped -77.9%. From that low point, it subsequently gained +70.3% (through 9/30/2004). Where does a -77.9% loss followed by a +70.3% gain leave the NASDAQ? Where would you guess? Even? Down 10%? The answer is down <u>62.4%</u> from its high. Gains and losses are not created equal.

✓ **RETIREMENT REALITY CHECK** ⟍

Decisive Action
The simple truth is risk changes over time. If you make a highly diversified investment in the stock market your risk of losing money <u>in the next five minutes</u> is pretty high. The risk of losing money the <u>next day</u> is still high. However, the risk of losing money over the next three years is lower and the risk of losing money over the next 25 years is lower still. Over longer time frames, risk changes radically.

Don't Get Burned Again!			
If Your Portfolio Lost...	Gains Needed to Break Even	The Time It Takes to Get Even at...	
		3%	6%
10%	11%	3.6 yrs.	1.8 yrs.
20%	25%	7.5 yrs.	3.8 yrs.
30%	43%	11.9 yrs.	6 yrs.
40%	67%	17 yrs.	8.6 yrs.
50%	100%	23.2 yrs.	11.6 yrs.

Not All Gains Are The Same: The Straight Line Mistake

A common mistake in planning for a lifetime of income is to base plans on historical averages and then project those averages out in linear fashion. You've seen and heard people do this. Now, referring to long-term averages does have some utility during the accumulation phase. It can serve as a lighthouse to encourage investors to look past the current stormy waters and continue on course.

But during the income phase, the seas are less forgiving. Options for correcting errors are more constrained. If the boat gets swamped on the beach before leaving for the voyage there is more hope of rescue. If the boat takes on water in the middle of the ocean, prospects for prosperity or survival are not as good.

When we look at average rates of return, it should be helpful to remember the following chart that illustrates four different portfolios. Consistent returns and compounding can have a dramatic impact on investments over time. Even though the average return is the same for all four portfolios after 20 years – it is10% – how the returns are achieved adds up to a difference of more than $53,0000 on an initial investment of $100,000.

✓ RETIREMENT REALITY CHECK

Decisive Action
A consistent investing strategy that seeks to avoid negative returns may prove to be more beneficial in the long run than aiming for sporadic short-term gains.

The Value of $100,000 Invested				
Year	**Portfolio A**	**Portfolio B**	**Portfolio C**	**Portfolio D**
1	10%	7%	20%	0%
2	10%	13%	20%	0%
3	10%	7%	20%	0%
4	10%	13%	20%	0%
5	10%	7%	20%	0%
6	10%	13%	20%	0%
7	10%	7%	20%	0%
8	10%	13%	20%	0%
9	10%	7%	20%	0%
10	10%	13%	20%	0%
11	10%	7%	0%	20%
12	10%	13%	0%	20%
13	10%	7%	0%	20%
14	10%	13%	0%	20%
15	10%	7%	0%	20%
16	10%	13%	0%	20%
17	10%	7%	0%	20%
18	10%	13%	0%	20%
19	10%	7%	0%	20%
20	10%	13%	0%	20%
Average	10%	10%	10%	10%
Geometric	10%	9.96%	9.54%	9.54%
Value	**$672,750**	**$667,763**	**$619,174**	**$619,174**

This chart is for illustrative purposes only and is not meant to predict or indicate future performance.
Past performance is no guarantee of future results.

✓   RETIREMENT REALITY CHECK   ↖

Realistic Expectations
Planning lifetime income on a linear projection of average returns can easily create a misleading sense of security or certainty about a portfolio's odds of success. The real world, as we all well know, is variable, unpredictable and does not travel in a straight line.

Taken a step further, suppose you make an investment that you plan on using in 5 years and you have a choice of account "A" or "B". Account B is about as exciting as watching paint dry but it will earn 8% annually. Account A will have the following returns: 20%, 21%, 10%, -17% and 10%. Which would you choose? Most people would pick account A if they didn't need the money for at least 5 years. But let's see what effect one losing year has on the overall return.

If you invested $100,000 today and had the following gains or losses, which would provide the highest balance in 5 years?		
	Option A	**Option B**
Year 1	+20%	+8%
Year 2	+20%	+8%
Year 3	+10%	+8%
Year 4	-17%	+8%
Year 5	+10%	+8%
TOTAL	$?	$?

The answer is actually Option B. It would have an ending balance of $146,932 versus Option A's ending balance of $145,824. And Option B had a little smoother ride along the way.

The Flaw of Averages: How To Go Broke Averaging 10.6% Annually

You've heard of the law of averages, but how often do you hear about the *flaw* of averages?

When "Lucky" Larry was getting ready to retire he visited the local soothsayer. The soothsayer informed him that the stock market (the S&P 500 index) would average 10.6% for precisely the next 40 years. Since Lucky had socked away one million dollars and had total confidence in the soothsayer's saying, he decided to withdraw $100,000 of income each year off of his portfolio—after all, that's just a 10% withdrawal rate from a portfolio he believed would average 10.6%. Lucky was confident in the soothsayer's prediction. Everything should be great. How did Lucky's portfolio look 40 years later? How much money did he have left?

The good news is Lucky did this in 1964. And the soothsayer was right! For the next 40 years the S&P 500 index did average 10.6%. Isn't that good news? Here's the bad news. Lucky went broke in 1981, less than 18 years later. His one million dollars was gone.

What happened? Lucky failed to recognize the difference between the market's actual year-to-year performance and its average performance. While the market did average 10.6% for the next 40 years, the market declines in the 1970s forced him to take his income from a smaller and smaller portfolio. When the market came back he had less principal in the market.

Lenny and Margaret

"Lucky" Lenny and Margaret the Market Maven both retired with a $500,000 account. They both decided to withdraw $25,000 per year and increase their income each year to adjust for inflation. Lenny visited the local soothsayer who told him that over the next 30 years he would make 7.5% every year except three. Not bad right? He would have 27 winning years and three losing years. In those three years he would have two years of 10% losses and one year of a 5% loss. The soothsayer told Lenny that Margaret would have the same return numbers, but the results may happen in different years.

Here's what happened. Lenny had his negative returns in the early years of retirement and then his investment made consistent 7.5% returns for the next 27 years. Margaret's investment got a consistent 7.5% return for 27 years and then she had her three negative years. There is no punch line because this isn't funny. Lenny went broke by the 19th year. Early negative returns caused him to eat into his principal in a compressed market. The long bull market gains didn't help him as much as it did Margaret because he had less principal at work. Even though both had investments that averaged 5.8% return, one person went broke and one didn't.

Having negative performance while taking income from a portfolio can be devastating. In the language stockbrokers speak, "stockbrokerese," there's special terminology to describe when this happens to someone. Are you ready? They say, "the account blew up." Lenny's account blew up.

The Risk of Experiencing Early Negative Returns!				
$25,000 Annual Income Inflation Adjusted Annuallly	**Early Market Decline "Lucky Lenny"**		**Late Market Decline Margaret "The Market Maven"**	
	Annual Return	Account Balance	Annual Return	Account Balance
Year 1	-10%	$427,500	7.5%	$510,625
Year 2	-10%	$361,575	7.5%	$521,241
Year 3	-5%	$318,300	7.5%	$531,822
Year 4	7.5%	$312,805	7.5%	$542,342
Year 5	7.5%	$306,018	7.5%	$552,769
Year 18	7.5%	$27,575	7.5%	$559,361
Year 19	7.5%	$0	7.5%	$563,060
Year 28	7.5%	$0	-5%	$556,612
Year 29	7.5%	$0	-10%	$449,473
Year 30	7.5%	$0	-10%	$351,503
Annualized 30-Year Return	5.8%		5.8%	

Source: The Vanguard Group

While averages may be statistically true, they can be moral lies. In other words, averages can be very misleading. Let me illustrate: The average family has 2.3 kids. Well, how many families do you know with 2.3 kids? If the average temperature in Nashville is 59.7 degrees (which it is), how many days can you count where the temperature all day is 59.7 degrees? None? Exactly. You get the point.

When Averages Don't Count

When we get to the income phase the rules change. We must realize that averages don't count – real results are what count. If history is any guide, and it's the only guide we have, let's take a look at the lessons of the past so we aren't doomed to repeat its mistakes.

Looking back from 1926 through the end of 2004, the S&P 500 stock index averaged about 10.4% annually[3]. But out of all those 79 years, how many times did it actually provide a calendar year return between 10% and 11%? Did you guess 20? 30? 10? Try one. Just one.

━━◀❏ WHAT DAD SAID ❐▶━━

Everything That Runs, Runs In Cycles

It has often occurred to me that when we, as a society and culture, moved away from an agrarian way of life we lost a real sense of cause and effect relationships and many of the cycles inherent in our world. My dad never lost sight of cycles.

One day while I was working on this book, I called dad. At some point in our conversation I said, "It's just a cycle." He said, "Everything that ever runs, runs in cycles." To that end, I noticed he'd buy convertibles during winter and sell them in the spring.

Is that too narrow of a band? Then let's find out how many times the market's return was between 8% and 12%. Surely 30 or 40 of those 78 years, right? Actually, the market's return was in the 8-12% range just four times. In fact, the market's loss was greater than 20% more times than it returned a gain of 8-12%. But that's only part of the story. The market's gain has been 20% or greater 31 times out of those 78 years.

The stock market is like electricity. If used prudently with the right risk management tools like insulation, regulators and wall sockets, you can have light to read a book at night, enjoy air-conditioning in the summer and listen to music on the radio. Using it without proper respect and understanding can give you quite a shock.

The stock market's returns don't go in a straight line – they never have. Expecting a return of 10-11% each year would've left you feeling a little off course 77 of those 78 years. So wouldn't using straight-line projections and calling that "financial planning" be insane? Yet we all did it before we knew

✓   RETIREMENT REALITY CHECK

Decisive Action
Because of the variability of returns with stocks, it makes sense to use tools and technology to manage that risk. We do things to manage the risk of owning a home by having homeowners insurance even though it's not very likely our house will burn down. We manage risk of owning a vehicle by having seat belts, airbags, antilock brakes and auto insurance. What are you doing to manage the risk of owning equities?

better. I did it early in my career. But now we know better. So let's not do that anymore.

The Siren Song of High Returns

What's more important: getting the highest rate of return or having the most money? Let me illustrate what I mean. Given the choice, which of the two investments would you choose? One that will go up 1% per year or one that will go up 50% one year and down 40% the next? The one with the big return sounds much sexier, doesn't it?

Let's figure it out. $100,000 makes 50% and becomes $150,000. The next year it loses 40% - that means we subtract $60,000. Now that $100,000 investment is worth only $90,000. It would have been better to earn a consistent 1%!

It's essential that we get a firm grasp on this concept. Too many folks are still randomly punching numbers on the phone – looking for 50% Nirvana. An income portfolio has to be designed for income. It's all about using the right vehicle to get the right job done. Remember, it's not what you make, it's what you keep that counts.

Just as it refers to life expectancy, we should look at probabilities for our individual situation – not just averages. To understand the importance

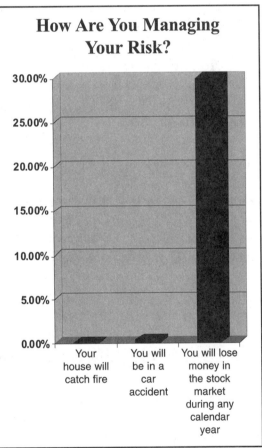

How Are You Managing Your Risk?

Source: Ibbotson Associates, Inc. based on the return of the S&P 500 Index from 1926-2003; About Long Term Care Insurance, Thomas Day. You cannot invest directly in an index.

of return patterns, suppose you held a mix of 60% stocks, 30% bonds and 10% treasury bills. If you held that mix over the 30 years that ended in 1998, you averaged a rate of return far above historical averages: you got a whopping 11.7% average annual return. But despite that good performance, the sustainable withdrawal rate was 5.8%[4]. Why only 5.8%? Because the early returns were so dismal that by the time the good times rolled around much of your principal would have been spent if you had withdrawn more (remember Lenny). And if you had done that, you would've had less money to reap the rewards of the up cycle of the market.

What if you put those returns in reverse? Imagine the same 30-year retirement, but the rate of the returns your first year in retirement for stocks, bonds and T-bills was like the return in 1998. Your second year mirrored 1997, your third year 1996 and went on back to 1969. According to T. Rowe Price's research, your portfolio could have sustained a 10.7% withdrawal rate.

The same years, same rates of return, just put in a different order made a 100% difference in the amount of income received without having the portfolio stressed-out.

How lucky do you feel? Doesn't it make sense to rely on something other than just hope?

Monte Carlo – It's Not Just For Gamblers Anymore

A few years ago many planners started using "Monte Carlo" simulations. Monte Carlo is a probability pattern generator that produced a range of possible results based on a given portfolio of assets. Instead of a single answer like "take 6% withdrawals and adjust them for inflation," a Monte Carlo simulation will examine hundreds of possible future outcomes for a portfolio. Usually the outcomes are based on a range of historical market actions. The output of Monte Carlo is a probability of reaching a goal based on historical market conditions using the current mix of investments.

Using straight-line analysis might say you could withdraw 8% and be fine. Monte Carlo may say that if you withdraw 8% there is a 59% chance of delivering income until age 90 but that probability may drop to 44% if you live to age 95. And that you have an 89% probability of generating income through age 81. Now the question becomes, "Are you willing to take a 41% chance of running out of money before age 90? How about a 56% chance of running out before 95? How about an 11% chance of running out before age 81? How lucky do you feel?" That's why it's called Monte Carlo.

Using this tool may give you a more clear understanding of how your current portfolio design may or may not work under a variety of situations.

Why Dollar-Cost-Averaging May Be A Great Idea

Dollar-cost-averaging means simply investing a fixed amount of money into an investment at regular intervals. It's what most people do in their 401(k), 403(b) or other company retirement plan. The concept is that by putting a fixed dollar amount into the investment more shares are purchased when the cost of the investment is low and fewer shares are purchased when the cost is high.

In a generally rising market this works great during accumulation and may work even better with more volatile investments. What are the risks? If you have a lump sum to invest all at one time you may miss out on some appreciation by not investing all at once when the price was low. In a declining market, you may lose whether you cost average or not.

Sue: Dollar-Cost-Averaging			
Month	Investment Amount	Unit Price	Units Purchased
January	$200	$10	20.0
February	$200	$9	22.2
March	$200	$6	33.4
April	$200	$8	25.0
May	$200	$11	9.1
TOTAL	$1,000		118.8

Dollar-Cost Averaging and other periodic investment plans do not assure a profit and do not protect against loss in declining markets. Since cost-averaging involves continuous investments regardless of fluctuating price levels, you should consider your financial ability to continue adding money through periods of low price levels before starting such a plan.

Let's use a hypothetical example. Bob and Sue both have $1,000 to invest. Bob invests $1,000 one time at $10 per unit so he owns 100 units of the investment at an average cost of $10 per unit. Sue decides to invest $200 per month over the next five months. Each month the investment fluctuates in value as shown. In this example, Bob made money but Sue made more. Bob's average cost per share is $10 while Sue's average cost per share is $8.42. The same dollar amount invested bought a whole lot more shares when the price was down. Of course if the investment had gone straight up, Bob would've made more money. Have you ever made an investment only to see it drop the next day? I have. You may want to remember Sue.

> "These days man knows the price of everything, but the value of nothing."
> – Oscar Wilde

Cost averaging can sometimes make even mediocre investments work well for you. The strategy can put volatility to work for you rather than having volatility work against you. Lucky Larry and Sue both anticipate having $100,000 per year to invest for the next 9 years. Lucky and Sue visited a soothsayer (a different one this time—at Larry's prompting) to help make a decision about their annual investment. There are two choices, both at $10 per share. The soothsayer says investment A will be $10 per share nine years from now and that investment B will be $18 per share in nine years. Assuming both Sue and Larry will be adding money each year and not withdrawing any, who will end up with more money in nine years?

Sue (Investment A)			
Year	Investment Amount	Unit Price	Units Purchased
1	$100,000	$10	10,000.000
2	$100,000	$8	12,500.000
3	$100,000	$6	16,666.667
4	$100,000	$4	25,000.000
5	$100,000	$2	50,000.000
6	$100,000	$4	25,000.000
7	$100,000	$6	16,666.667
8	$100,000	$8	12,500.000
9	$100,000	$10	10,000.000
TOTAL	$900,000		178,333.333
ENDING VALUE	$1,783,333.33	$5.05/unit avg.	

Lucky Larry (Investment B)			
Year	**Investment Amount**	**Unit Price**	**Units Purchased**
1	$100,000	$10	10,000.000
2	$100,000	$11	9,090.909
3	$100,000	$12	8,333.333
4	$100,000	$13	7,692.308
5	$100,000	$14	7,142.857
6	$100,000	$15	6,666.667
7	$100,000	$16	6,250.000
8	$100,000	$17	5,882.353
9	$100,000	$18	5,555.556
TOTAL	$900,000		66,613.982
ENDING VALUE	**$1,199,051.68**	**$13.51/unit avg.**	

How did Sue end up with almost $600,000 more than Larry? After Larry left the Soothsayer's high-rise office, Sue stayed to ask some more questions. It wasn't just the investment's performance that dictated Sue's success; Sue's behavior was a major contributor. Larry got the 'right' answer but he asked the wrong question. He climbed the ladder of success leaning against the wrong wall.

Now let's move this into a more real world example. What do you think Sue actually would've done in the above example? After five years of losing money do you think she would keep putting money into the investment? Or would it be more likely that she would've sold out of investment A close to the bottom and switched over to investment B (or, even more likely, just stopped investing altogether and stuffed the money under the mattress where inflation would eat it down to nothing).

✓	RETIREMENT REALITY CHECK	⌐

Knowledge
The same reason dollar-cost-averaging can work so well during the accumulation phase is the same reason it can be such a hideous strategy during the distribution phase. When we begin taking income from the portfolio, we don't want to HAVE to sell more shares when the market is down to maintain our income.

We've dealt with cost averaging during the accumulation phase – that's what is frequently promoted in the investment community. But what happens when we make the transition to income? Do the rules change?

Why Dollar-Cost-Averaging May Be A BAD Idea

Dollar-cost-averaging is like a cup of water. The cup is open at the top and closed at the bottom and it holds the water in. It works that way. That's how a cup is to be used. That's accumulation—when we're filling the cup up. But now try to use a cup with the closed part at the top and the opening at the bottom. You end up with a wet floor. That's the distribution or income phase. An upside down a cup doesn't work.

If we enter the income phase with an accumulation phase mentality, the results can be disastrous. The cup is upside down. If we enter the spending phase with a reverse dollar-cost-average strategy, taking sizeable equal installments out of a volatile investment, we have virtually no strategy at all. Let's consider the same illustration that we used before, but now let's look at taking money out instead of investing money back in.

It's not hard to see that the same reason cost averaging may work during accumulation may be the same reason it could spell o-u-c-h when we start taking income.

It comes down to this basic question: Is your investment vehicle designed specifically for your purpose?

Why Investor Behavior May Be More Important Than Investment Performance

There is a huge gap between the way investments perform and the results people get. Look at the phenomenal difference that exists between *investment* performance and *investor* performance. That statement may sound like nonsense, so let's be clear on the difference. Investment performance is just a ratio: the price of the investment at the beginning of the period compared to the price of it end of the period. Investor performance measures when individuals actually put money to work and when they cashed out.

In his book, *One Up On Wall Street,* Peter Lynch tells that during his tenure as manager of one of the country's most successful investment companies for two decades, about one out of three investors lost money. In the book he relays the story of the days in October 1987 that he had to sell billions of dollars of stocks when the market was compressed because of investors wanting to cash out.

Now, let's think back to Sue's example of dollar-cost-averaging with the investment that went from $10 down to $2 and back up to $10. From the starting date, how good was "investment perform-ance?" It was terrible, wasn't it? It went no-where. What if she made a one-time invest-ment? She would've made no money over a nine-year period (assum-ing of course there were no dividends reinvest-

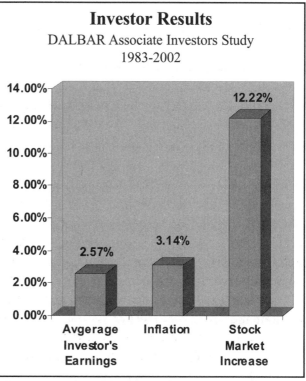

Investor Results

DALBAR Associate Investors Study
1983-2002

ed). The "investment" made no money. Think about it. In the example we used, the "investment" did terribly. But using the dollar-cost-averaging strat-egy with that terribly volatile investment, the "investor" did great. It was the investor's behavior that had a significant impact on the outcome. Remember though, dollar-cost-averaging is no guarantee of success nor a guarantee against a loss.

Think about Lucky Larry. He had an investment that did reasonably well and he used the same strategy. Even though the investor's behavior was the same, the investment did better, but the investor ended up with less money.

Larry had the investment with the highest rate of return but Sue made the most money. So should we be more concerned about the highest rate of investment return or having the most money? It's obvious, isn't it? If we're always looking for the highest rate of return then we're not answering the right question.

From 1984 to 2000, the S&P 500 averaged 16.29% annually. During this time of phenomenal growth the average investor in a domestic equity fund realized an annual return of 5.32%[5]. In another recent three-year period ending in 2001, Financial Planning Interactive concluded in a period of time where the average equity investment's return was 10.9% annually that the average dollar invested earned just 8.7%.

The investing public is chasing performance. And it's not working for them.

Information Overload and Its Consequence: Chasing Performance

Every day you are surrounded by "financial pornography." The information is everywhere, it's tantalizing, it's cheap, it seems like it's just for you, it doesn't really get you anywhere, and it can get you all excited with nothing to do about it.

When you think about magazines, television shows, newspapers, websites and radio shows, what do they have in common? Their revenue is derived from advertising. It's simple; if more people tune in then ads sell for more money. How do you get more people to tune in and turn on? How about tapping into the emotion of fear? Why not touch the hot button of greed?

☞ CAN YOU IMAGINE: ☜
Information Vs. Knowledge

Sally is an M.D. and Ph.D. at a major research hospital. She is distinguished among her peers for her innovative and meticulous work with infectious diseases. To say she is bright would be an understatement. Every month deductions from her income are put into her retirement plan at the hospital. Sally confessed that after two decades of putting money into the market, for the past several years into an indexed investment, that she couldn't take the volatility anymore, so at the end of 2002 she moved everything into the fixed account. "At least it's safe, right?" Of course the S&P subsequently rose over 28% in 2003.

I am not trying to belabor the point, I just want to make sure this isn't just information. I want to make sure it makes the critical jump from information to knowledge and that you know it so well you can and will act on it. And it's hard. It's very simple, but it's hard. So many people want to think they invest long-term, but the facts don't bear that out.

Information is not the key. Sally has loads of information. Intelligence is not the key. Sally has gobs of intelligence. It takes knowledge, a plan and appropriate action.

Media companies know this. That's why one month the magazine sells greed on its cover. The next month it sells fear. "You have to have this information." "Tune in tonight to find out why the market declined dramatically. Where should you invest for profits in the New Year? Find out from our experts. You can't retire without it. You have to watch the show tomorrow."

In 1996, the Internet was in its infancy and about the only financial news show that had any following that I knew of was Louis Reukeyser, who was on once a week. The average holding period for long-term was 5.5 years. By 2002 everyone had access to stock quotes on the Internet, there were entire cable networks dedicated to financial news and the holding period had shortened to less than 3 years.[6]

In 2003, an update to Dalbar's Quantitative Analysis of Investor Behavior study showed that since 1984 equity investors have held their investments for just over 2 years on average. And most have earned less than the rate of inflation.

The average equity investor earned 2.57% annually; inflation ran at an average of 3.14%; and the S&P 500 index averaged 12.22% over that same period. The average fixed income investor did slightly better at 4.24% annually compared to the 11.70% average return of the Lehman Long-term Government Bond index. Keep in mind that you cannot invest directly in an index.

In their study, Dalbar concluded, despite what advertisements may have us believe, that "a one size fits all solution is not the answer." That's not a real shocker, is it?

The disparity between investment performance and investor performance was pointed out in the April, 1997 issue of *Money* magazine. The study showed the results of the investments and the average results for the shareholders. One investment was up over +20% for the year but the average shareholder lost over -30%. Another investment cited was up over +26% while the average shareholder was down −20%. The difference exists because the average investor invests once the price has risen and then gets out when it declines. Of course, this isn't always the case, but it is a good example of an all-too-frequent behavior.

Information is random, chaotic and miscellaneous. Knowledge on the other hand is orderly, cumulative and focused.

Taking advice from someone who doesn't know you, your values, goals, objectives, dreams – in essence what's really important to you – is more like taking a prescription from a physician who's never met you and doesn't know anything about you. It's more like an addiction or a bet than a sound financial decision.

Insights to Investor Behavior: Same As It Ever Was

From: *Mood and Root of the Plunge*

"It was such a vast bull market, rising so spectacularly, that anybody with eyes was bound to see it, and anyone with a normal quota of human greed was bound to hanker to climb aboard. Over the past eight years, millions of new investors jumped into the market for shares listed on the New York Stock Exchange. When they ran out of growth stocks on the Big Board or the American Stock Exchange, people turned to the new issues traded over the counter. There were new companies with untried management, small earnings and dubious prospects – with nothing but a prayer and a catchy space age name – which were bid up as much as 400% within a few months… 'The reason stocks are so popular,' one securities analyst said, 'is that we've got a whole new generation of investors who don't know that stocks can do you dirt. … a market analyst said self-critically, 'the trouble was that we got away from any real study of securities values.' …It's too early to say whether the bull market has ended or not, but it's certainly ended for some of the stocks that got out of line."

Life Magazine, Summer 1962, upon the plunge of the Dow
from its high of 700 to around 550 on May 28, 1962.

Past Performance Is No Guarantee of Future Results

If information overload doesn't lead to paralysis it certainly temps us into chasing performance. Almost all of us have done it at some point in life. You read the disclaimer "past performance is no guarantee of future success." Does anyone really believe that? People have the information that past performance is no guarantee, but do they know it? Do they act on it?

Have you ever gotten financial "tips" that you've acted on? Someone on the airplane mentioned a stock that was going to "take off." Someone on TV or on the golf course said a company was going to blast off, or a stockbroker cold-called you with a "hot tip."

I would submit to you there is no more misunderstood phrase in the investment lexicon than "past performance is no guarantee of future results."

I cannot count the times someone has sat in my office and said, "I know past performance is no guarantee of future results, but how has this done?" We want to know. There's something basically human about the inquiry.

Let's look at history for some insight. If we look at different types of investments that performed well over a five year period and then looked at their performance over the next five years we see a startling revelation. We see that past performance is no guarantee of future results! Looking at the various segments of the market gives us some insight. Let's consider some of the sectors of the stock market in 1999 and their subsequent performance. Technology companies as a whole had a

It's Like This

DRIVING WHILE LOOKING IN THE REAR VIEW MIRROR

Imagine you're driving down I-65 at 65 miles per hour, both hands firmly on the steering wheel. Now lean up real close to the rear view mirror so that your eyes are about 4 inches from the mirror. You have a great view behind you but you can't see anything in front of you. Now imagine trying to drive like that all the time. How well does it work? Of course it doesn't. We don't do it when we're driving because it would be too dangerous. We look ahead. That's what looking only at past performance is like. Looking at past performance is like driving while looking in the rear view mirror.

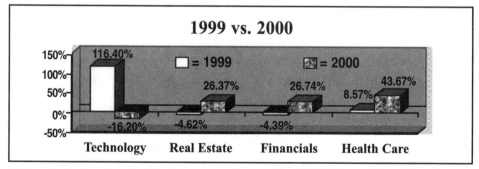

Benchmark data taken from the following unmanaged indexes: The NAREIT (National Association of Real Estate Investment Trust) Equity Index, a representative of real estate investment trusts; Lipper Health/Biotechnology Fund Index, a representative of health care and biotech stock funds; PSE Technology Index, a representative of technology stocks; Lehman Brothers Aggregate Bond Index, a representative of U.S. government and corporate bonds. Results are based on total returns and include reinvestment of dividends.

great year in 1999 and they dominated the headlines in the year 2000. Yet health care, bonds and real estate were wonderful performers. Go back to the mainstream financial press of 1999 and see just how much space was being given to the under-performers of '99-not much.

Consider the portion of the market usually called "large company growth stocks" (the S&P / Barra 500 Growth Index). During the five-year period of 1995-1999 it was the best performing major U.S. equity indices. During the subsequent five years, 2000-2004, it was one of the worst performing. The Russell 2000 Value Index was one of the worst performing in 1998 and 1999 logging losses of -6.45% and -1.49%. However, the next two years delivered returns of +22.83% followed by +14.02%. During those two years the S&P 500 showed losses of -9.11%

Captain Kirk or Mr. Spock?

We know that change is constant in life, in economics and the markets. And every one of us is human. These two basic factors – change and human emotions – are continually at work. There seems to be Mr. Spock and a Captain Kirk inside each of us. One part is purely rational and the other part makes decisions from the heart. If we make decisions based purely on emotion we run the risk of being caught up in the emotional cycle of investing when things get tough. And we know there will be times when things get tough. We have to make certain that we have a plan to deal with the ups and downs so we can continue to boldly go where we have never gone before.

Investing without a plan, based on emotion and hope doesn't usually lead to stellar results.

The Buy-and-Hold Lie

Will Rogers said, "Buy a good stock. When it goes up sell it. If it doesn't go up, don't buy it." It would be nice if we could invest with 20/20 hindsight. But since that will never happen we must have a process for selecting a time to buy, a time to hold 'em and a time to fold 'em.

It's so easy to focus on the investments rather than the process. To be successful we must focus on the process. I have several friends in manufacturing businesses from computer chips to automobiles. They will tell you that quality and consistency doesn't come from a one-time decision that you put on autopilot. It comes from a vigorous and consistent process. It's all about the process.

It's a beautiful idea to think that all you really have to do is buy a good company's stock and never sell to get super rich. But the facts don't bear it out any more than the certainty that the road to financial success is to bet on red 27 at the roulette table. "Buy and never sell" is a first cousin to "plant and never prune or fertilize." It would be nice if life worked like that, but it doesn't.

The Emotional Cycle of Investing

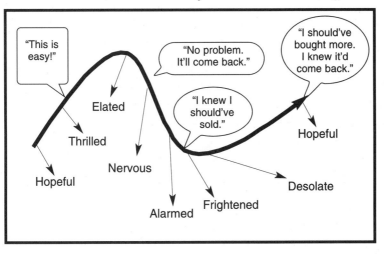

Virtually no blue chip company stays a blue chip forever. Even great companies can stumble and fall, and they frequently do. When Charles Dow created the Dow Jones Average in 1885, there were 14 companies in his index. Of the 14 original companies only one is still around today. Look at recent history with companies like Pan American World Airways, Woolworth, Kmart, Bethlehem Steel, Enron, WorldCom and Service Merchandise.

Bethlehem steel was a blue chip and part of the Dow Jones Industrial Average well into the 1990s. Fortunes were made with American steel. But things change. Had you bought the company in 1957 with the idea that you never sell anything, you would've seen your blue chip go from over $90 per share down and never get close to $90 over the next four decades. If you bought Microsoft or Cisco when most people had never heard of them you did very well. If you invested when they had been coined "one decision stocks," stocks that you buy and never have to make the decision to sell, you would've lost a great deal of money.

Most things have a life cycle and so do companies. The great companies can reinvent themselves and adjust to changes. Most companies don't. As investors we must have a process to distinguish between the two.

The Truth About Stock Market Returns

If we look at the way the market really cycles we get a different perspective than what is often paraded before the public.

If we track the Dow Jones Industrial Average from 1901 through 2004, we see that the market spent about 23% of its time making "new wealth," that

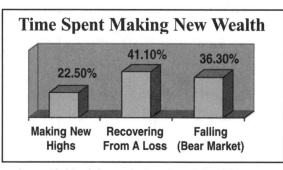

Source: Ned Davis Research. Dow Jones Industrial Average
6/17/1901 - 09/30/2004

is, reaching new highs. Over 41% of the time has been spent recovering from losses and fully 36% of the time has been spent in "bear markets." If we are concerned about growing our money, we could always "ride it out." If we need income from the portfolio, we need some sort of risk management tool, process or protocol to give us some shock absorbers.

The good news is that tools are available in a variety of forms. Wouldn't it make sense to apply some process so you improve your odds of making new money and keeping what you've made?

Diversification

"Tis the part of a wise man to keep himself today for tomorrow, and not venture all his eggs in one basket." — Cervantes

There are a number of strategies you can use to protect your money and improve the consistency of your returns. Diversification is just one smart way to help. Nobel prize-winning Modern Portfolio theory states in a very fancy and eloquent way a truth we all knew all along anyway: Don't put all your eggs in one basket.

It's doubtful that anyone would question the wisdom of 'don't put all your eggs in one basket.' The saying has certainly stood the test of time since Cervantes came up with the metaphor more than 400 years ago. A few centuries later we've come up with the fifty-cent term: asset allocation.

What is asset allocation? It is the process of dividing your money among different asset classes so your investments are well diversified. Asset allocation is simply making sure all your eggs aren't in the same basket.

"By strategically diversifying your assets you help offset declines in any one particular class, and have the potential to smooth out the ups and downs of your portfolio and reduce risk over the long term... Research shows that it is the asset allocation decision that accounts for more than 90% of the variation between returns in different investment portfolios." [7]

I haven't won many Nobel Prizes lately, so I can't dispute whether asset allocation is 91% or 89% or even 80% of the determining force. But I do know that if you want to maintain your lifestyle over a long period of retirement, you have to make sure your mix of investments is uniquely suited for your intended purpose.

> "You can become wealthy by underdiversifying. You cannot stay wealthy by underdiversifying."

Keeping too many assets in a money market or bond account can cause a person to drastically reduce their lifestyle due to the usual loss of purchasing power over time. Too many assets in stocks or having too high of a withdrawal rate during the spending phase can over-stress a portfolio beyond its ability to deliver.

Make sure you consult with a qualified professional in this area. It's easy to own five or even ten different investments and think you're diversified. Don't fall into the trap of believing that just because you own several different investments that there is diversification. Investments of one type tend to rise and fall together. You need a mix of investments to help work toward consistency of returns.

Tactical vs. Static

When it comes to approaches to asset allocation you have two main processes you can employ, tactical or static allocation.

A manager that uses a tactical approach will change the concentrations of investments between cash, bonds and different segments of the market depending upon economic and market conditions and will move in and out of different types of assets. A tactical manager may have a heavy weighting in blue chip stocks and small company stocks one year and be heavily weighted in interna-

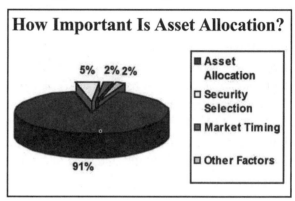

Gary P. Brinson, L. Randolph Hood and Gilbert L. Beebower

tional investments and bonds the next in an effort to protect principal and own whatever is working now. The tactical manager is the pastor of the church of "what's happening now."

☞ CAN YOU IMAGINE: ☜
Fake Diversification

Carol is a successful business owner who called an advisor because she was disgusted with the results of her company's 401(k). The advisor went through all the elements and considerations of the plan. It seemed that everything was in order until he got down to the investment choices. Like most company retirement plans there was a menu of about 15 choices. Twelve of those choices had virtually identical returns! Even though they all had different names and were from different managers, they were virtually identical. No wonder Carol and her employees were unhappy. As the advisor talked about the process of selecting which 15 investments got included, Carol revealed that the investments had been selected based on their previous 5-year track record, which was good (and virtually identical).

When the new advisor took the plan over they simply got rid of nine of the look-alikes and replaced them with truly diversified investments. To everyone in the plan it had looked like they were well diversified, but they weren't.

The drawback of tactical is that a manager may make a wrong allocation decision. She may be invested in small company stocks when international stocks is the place to be; he may be heavily allocated to cash when bonds are the "hot" asset.

Static allocation is the approach that says no matter what is going on today, let's use a fixed mixture: maybe 60% stocks and 40% bonds for example. Within the stock allocation 10% may be committed to international investments and 40% to blue chip stocks. Static allocation is an "all-weather" investment approach. It's like dressing for an average temperature of 59.7 degrees whether it's winter, spring, summer or fall.

Unless a manager is specified as a tactical manager, they are probably static. They may have a name like a large cap growth manager or a small cap value manager or a large cap growth and income manager. They have a specific mandate and will manage the best they can within that specialty.

Which approach is right for you? That's for you and your advisor to determine. Both approaches have their appeal. You may even want to use a combination of approaches so you are not only diversifying your assets but also diversifying the strategies used to decide on the specific investments.

Another Word About Risk

It may be okay to take risks that we know about. It's not a good plan to take risks we don't even know we are taking. For example, in the mid-to-late 1990s many people stopped viewing technology stocks as risky. Some of them, like Cisco Systems or Nortel or Lucent Technologies, were even called "one decision stocks" – stocks you could make the decision to buy and never have to make a decision to sell. That didn't work out so well.

One of the things I have heard with increasing frequency over the past several years, is "you only lose money if you sell it." Isn't that one of the most ridiculous things you've ever heard? I understand the principal behind not panicking out of great investments when they are down, but to say you didn't lose money on a losing investment just because you didn't sell is to voluntarily separate yourself from reality. Try using that "no loss" logic on those poor people who bought Enron (believing the earnings were real) and didn't sell – try to tell them they didn't lose money. It's crazy.

Index or Indices?

An index is simply a benchmark or a measuring stick to give us a point of reference for measuring. The atomic clock at Los Alamos gives us a benchmark against which we can all set our watches.

Perhaps the most widely recognized financial index is the Dow Jones Industrial Average. Created by Charles Dow in 1885, the index was originally composed of 14 stocks, most of which were railroad stocks. It was a reflection of the economy of the day. As a financial journalist, Dow created the index to measure the stock market's performance and used it in the publication he started in 1889 called *The Wall Street Journal*. The Dow now consists of 30 companies generally referred to as "blue chip" companies. Only one of the original 14 remains (General Electric). Periodically, the index is adjusted to try to maintain a consistent representation of the U.S. economy. Among others, in the 1990s Wal-mart, Intel and Microsoft were added to the average as companies such as Bethlehem Steel, Woolworth and Westinghouse were removed.

There are a number of different indices. Some of the more common market indices you may hear or read about are:

- Dow Jones Industrial Average
- S&P 500
- Nasdaq composite
- Barra 400 Value
- Barra 400 Growth
- Russell 1000
- Russell 3000
- MSCI EAFE
- Wilshire 1000

Each of the different sectors of the market has an index. Some examples of this are:

- Technology Index
- Consumer Durables Index
- Utilities Index

Different indices have different tendencies or "behaviors." A bond index tends to have much less fluctuation than a technology stock index. A small company index may go up while a large company index goes down.

Most popular indices are weighted by capitalization. Capitalization, or "cap," is simply the total value of the company. Capitalization is calculated by multiplying the total number of shares by the stock price. A company with a stock price of $10 per share with 100,000 shares outstanding would have a market cap of $1 million.

What does that mean to us? With capitalization-weighted indices the larger companies have significantly more impact on the index. That can mean that most of the movement in an index is due to just a handful of stocks. Few indexes are equal weighted. The difference between capitalization weighting and equal weighting is like the difference between the House of Representatives and the Senate. In fact, in the S&P 500 the difference between the largest and smallest company may be a difference of more than 300 times. Therefore what happens with a handful of the largest companies has more impact on the index than what happens with the smallest 200 companies out of the 500. Of course, you cannot invest directly in an index.

Over the course of time some indexes may become very concentrated. For example, in the spring of 2000, the concentration in technology stocks in the S&P 500 was up to almost 40% at the height of the technology bubble.

It's Like This

RIDE WHAT'S RIGHT FOR YOU

When I was a kid I didn't play or watch basketball or baseball with my dad. Our activity was Sunday afternoon motorcycle rides through the woods and fields around our house. For several years I rode a Honda trail bike with a four-stroke engine. The power was smooth, the sound was mellow and the torque it developed at low rpms was good for learning and the slower speeds at which I rode. Eventually, I began riding faster and harder and the suspension would bottom out frequently as I landed from jumps. My bike was designed for smooth power delivery for moderate trail riding, not thrashing.

Then I bought a liquid cooled Honda CR125 - a motocross racing cycle. I had it bored and stroked and installed a high-compression Wiseco piston. It was a fire-breather. It probably had three times the horsepower of my previous 125. In biker lingo it had a "narrow powerband." That means that unlike my mellow four-stroke, where you could take off at low rpms and gradually increase the throttle, this bike had to be revved up high. There was hardly any horsepower until you got up to at least 8,000 rpms - higher than I rode the four-stroke. On take-off the choice was to start with low rpms and risk having the engine die or leaning over the front handlebars to try to keep the front wheel close to the ground. It was a lot faster, but it was really hard to ride slow enough to pick your way through dense woods. The sound was piercing and the horsepower took serious concentration to control. But it had gobs of suspension to help handle the higher speeds the bike could deliver.

The difference between the two bikes was like the difference between large stocks (blue chip stocks) and small company stocks. Small company stocks may travel faster at times, but you better have lots of suspension to enjoy the ride. Blue chip stocks may not always travel as fast, but they aren't as likely to give you a scary ride. Just like the cycles, each one works better when it is put to the right use.

Pulling It All Together

Let's pull the information in this section together. First, stocks can be a great investment to help us maintain our purchasing power and by staying ahead of inflation over the long haul. Second, because of the unpredictable short-term returns of stocks, using stocks for short-term income needs can create a genuine problem. Some of the strategies we used during the growth phase, such as dollar-cost-averaging, can actually work against us during the income phase. Investor behavior can have as much, or more, impact on results as investment performance.

The process for selecting investments is they key element. We must use good risk management tools to help us prune, fertilize and maximize the yield of our financial crop.

The bottom line is this: a beautifully managed portfolio of great companies can do wonders for us in the long haul, but we must have efficacious strategies to deal with the volatility over the short term. Stocks may have the engine of a great investment vehicle, but we've got to have a good pair of shock absorbers to enjoy the ride.

SUMMING IT UP

o   Risk changes over time. The longer period of time we're dealing with, the more we have to be aware of risks other than day-to-day fluctuations in market value of investments.

o   Over the long haul, it has been much more profitable to be an owner of great businesses than to be a loaner to great businesses.

o   A consistent investing strategy that seeks to avoid negative returns may prove to be more beneficial in the long run than aiming for sporadic short-term gains.

o   Markets don't move in straight lines - therefore, Boomers need to manage fluctuations during the income stage of their financial lives.

o   Dollar-cost-averaging has been a good tool for Boomers to use when growing their portfolio; it could be disastrous when they are taking out income.

o   Investing suffers when we invest our emotions in the process.

1- Federal Reserve Board

2 - Ibbottson Associates, Inc.

3 - Ibid

4 - T. Rowe Price

5 - Dalbar, Inc. Quantitative Analysis of Investor Behavior, June 21, 2001

6 - Financial Research Corporation

7 - Gary P. Brinson, L. Randolph Hood and Gilbert L. Beebower. "Determinants of Portfolio Performance"/Financial Analysts Journal May/June 1991

Chapter 6
TAKING CARE OF CARE TAKING

Confronting Long-Term Health Care

"It is a strange anomaly that men should be careful to insure their houses, their ships, and their merchandise, and yet neglect to insure their lives; surely the most important of all to their families and more subject to loss."
— Benjamin Franklin

What are your plans once your health fails? It's all too easy to skim over that question and not answer it. Yet one of the biggest challenges to anyone's financial health is funding lifetime quality care without demolishing your portfolio and ultimately your lifestyle. Do you have a written plan? Are your intentions in writing?

Do you have long-term care insurance? Most people don't. And why is that? There are basically two answers to that question. Number one, "it" will never happen to them and number two, it's too expensive. Let's talk straight, look at the facts and then you decide what makes sense.

When you think about the threats to your retirement savings most people usually think about market losses. Oftentimes, it is not market related events but catastrophic life events, like illness, that wreak havoc on retirement savings.

✓   RETIREMENT REALITY CHECK

Realistic Expectations
There are basically two phases to retirement. The first phase is the active phase, filled with traveling, taking care of grandkids, doing things for other people. The second phase, is the healthcare phase. Study after study has shown that we Americans spend roughly 80% of all our healthcare dollars in our last year of life. Healthcare can be very expensive.

If you had a spouse or family member that needed healthcare, how much of your retirement would you be willing to spend to help that person? All of it? I would too.

When it comes to dealing with the healthcare risk late in your life, you have two choices. Number one, you can self-insure or number two, you can reinsure. Those are your only two options. You can hold the risk yourself or you can spread the risk around. If you don't have long term care insurance you are self-insuring and you have to ask yourself an important question: can you afford to foot the bill out of your retirement nest egg? Would there be any financial strain if your expenses went up $60,000 or $90,000 or even $120,000 per year over what you anticipate? If you haven't reinsured, no one else will pick up the bill for most long-term care.

What is Long-Term Care?

Long-term care (LTC for short) is insurance that can pay for assistance once we need help with Activities of Daily Living (ADLs). It helps cover your risk should you need help in your home, in an assisted living facility or, even as a last resort, a nursing home.

As we learned earlier, there is an increasing probability that we will live a life long past the "life expectancy" we grew up with. With that longer life may come things we don't expect – "life unexpectancies," if you will. Haven't there been changes with you as you've gotten older that you didn't expect? There have been for me. Twenty years ago no one could have made me believe that the hair that grew from the top of my head and extended well past my shoulders would stop growing and and fall out and instead hair would start growing inside my ears! Maybe it's something different for you, but the fact is that our bodies change as we get older. Like a local celebrity once said, "Anyone who says they can do the same things at 50 that they did at 25, just didn't do a heck of a lot at 25!"

What Is The Risk?

A major risk to your retirement income is the potential for a catastrophic healthcare event to wipe out your retirement nest egg and deteriorate your standard of living or standard of care. If you're married, having something happen to you could jeopardize your spouse's financial security if you don't properly have your risk covered. The average annual cost for a skilled care facility is over $40,000 in the state of Tennessee but varies from state to state. And that is the average. Would you be comfortable with the average? In-home assistance can be significantly more expensive. If one spouse out of a couple had the need for care, would an extra $40,000 to $80,000 per year in expenses affect their lifestyle?

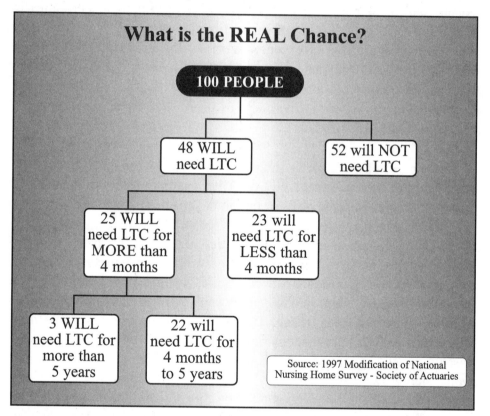

How Will You Pay for Long-Term Care?

One choice you may have is public programs like Medicare. Provided you meet certain strict criteria, Medicare may pay some costs for the first three months. However, 91.5% of nursing home costs are *not* paid by Medicare.

You don't want to rely on Medicaid. In order to qualify, you have to spend down your assets to the state's poverty level. It is now a crime to give away assets to a family member in order to qualify for Medicaid. It could take years to qualify and would be devastating to your family's finances.

You could rely on your family or your kids. After all, you took care of your kids; they owe you something, don't they? Oh, neither you nor your kids want that? I don't blame you.

If you don't have coverage, you are self-insured. You have assumed all the risk on yourself. And you need to consider that health care costs have been rising, and will probably continue to rise. Since 1970, health care costs have risen 4.6 to 6 percentage points faster than inflation.[1]

It's imperative that we face the truth about this issue. If you can handle the extra expense, no problem, you don't need insurance. Someone with very little in assets will qualify for Medicaid governmental support once they "spend down" their assets to virtually nothing. It's all the people IN THE MIDDLE that have something to lose. If you're in the middle, you need to consider reinsuring at least part of your risk. It is as simple as that.

It Will Never Happen To Me

Forty-three percent of Americans age 65 or older will spend some time in a nursing home and nearly eight million Americans are receiving some form of long-term health care today.[2] Seven in 10 couples (65 and older) can expect one spouse to need long term care.[3] And yet, in a recent survey by the American Health Care Association, 76% of the people surveyed said they do not expect to need long-term care in the future. There is a tremendous disconnect between the expectations and the facts.

Consider the facts:

• You have a 43% likelihood of being in a nursing home at least once during your lifetime. Half of nursing home stays are short, usually three months or less, so you have only a 23% likelihood of staying in

---

✓ **RETIREMENT REALITY CHECK** ⬆

Realistic Expectations
    On a nationwide basis, Medicare only covers about 8.5% of nursing home care costs each year. (Source: Facts and Trends, American Health Care Assoc., 1997, Health Care Financing Administration OSCAR 1/31/97).

a nursing home for more than a year, and a 9% likelihood of staying more than five years.[4]

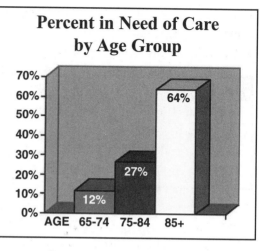

Source: General Electric Publication

- According to the New England Journal of Medicine, 43% of 65 year olds will need long-term care at some point during their retirement.
- More people are choosing to receive care at home. More than 83% of people with long-term care needs live in the community.[5]
- Options to receive community-based care are increasing. Between 1998 and 2000 the number of assisted living and board and care facilities increased from 24,572 to 32,886 nationally, reflecting the trend toward community-based care as opposed to nursing homes.[6]
- Average nursing home stays are less than five years. The average length of time since admission for current nursing home residents was 892 days (2.4 years).[7]
- Long-term care is not just for the old. Nearly 10 million people need long-term care – that is they need help with ADLs or IADLs. Most are age 65 or older, but 37% are under age 65.[8]
- About half of all claimants and informal caregivers indicated that, without private insurance, they would have to seek institutional alternatives – nursing home care or assisted living facilities.[9]

It's Too Expensive

Is your homeowners insurance or car insurance too expensive? Of course it is, unless you need it. Everyday your house doesn't burn down you've "wasted" money on homeowners insurance. Every day you don't have a car accident you've "wasted" money on auto insurance. And if you're alive to read this, you "wasted" money today on life insurance. But seriously, most of us don't wake up in the morning upset that our house didn't burn down or come home from work upset that we didn't have an auto accident so our insurance can pay off.

Risks In Your Life	Chance of Occurrence	Are You Insured?
House Burning	1 in 240	Yes
Car Accident	1 in 8	Yes
Medical Problem	Yearly	Yes
Long-Term Health	43 in 100	NO

Sources: 2001 National Safety Council; March 31, 2000 National Fire Prevention Assoc.;
1997 Modification of National Nursing Home Survey – Soc. Of Actuaries

We should all hope that we "waste" every penny we ever paid for insurance. All insurance is "wasted" money as long as we don't need it. And it is best to keep it that way. Covering your LTC risk may be less expensive than you thought.

Basic Concepts

There are four basic moving parts that affect the cost of a traditional long-term care policy. They are:

- Elimination Period – how long from the time you start needing it until it starts paying
- Coverage Period – the length of time the coverage will pay benefits
- Benefit Amount – how much it will pay per day or per month
- Riders – These can range from inflation riders (how much the amount of coverage will go up each year to cover increases in cost of living), to indemnity to cover additional costs of medication, return of premium rider which may return what you paid to your heirs in the event you don't use the benefit in your lifetime, as well as many others.

These four basic moving parts can be adjusted to design a cost-effective way to cover much of the risk associated with the need for this kind of care.

Elimination Period

This is the amount of time before coverage kicks in. Typically you'll have a choice of periods like 30, 60, 90 days or longer. Some people mistakenly think that Medicare will automatically cover the first 100 days. Don't be so certain. Less than 5% of families needing long-term care ever collect from Medicare because very specific criteria must be met in order to qualify (imagine that!).

When you evaluate the elimination period that's right for you, consider how long you would be willing or able to cover the costs with your own assets before coverage kicks in. The longer the elimination period – the more time spent paying on your dime – the lower the cost for insurance. The elimination period is like the deductible on your homeowners insurance. So one way to lower the cost is to increase the deductible – in other words, lengthen the elimination period.

One word of caution here. Make sure you're working with a qualified professional when looking into this kind of coverage. Here's why: Different companies have different ways of defining the elimination period. The easiest way to understand this may be through an example.

Suppose you have coverage with a 30-day elimination period

It's Like This

WHY BOOMERS DON'T HAVE LONG TERM CARE INSURANCE – BUT SHOULD

Much of what we learn about money we probably learned from our parents. As long as you own a car and a house I'm certain you have auto and homeowners insurance. Our parents had auto and homeowners insurance, no questions asked. But did they have long-term care insurance? Probably not. Because in their generation it was much less common. When cars were first introduced on the road auto insurance wasn't as common. Sixty years ago there wasn't a nursing home or an assisted living facility in every town. Previous generations didn't live as long. Congratulations, we are now experiencing the first of a massive demographic change that will require us to deal with the tremendous changes at hand.

and you got in a situation where you needed some help, say someone coming to your home three days a week to provide treatment for two hours a day and this started on January 1st. Common sense would say that your long-term care coverage would start paying for your care at the beginning of February. Right? Well, maybe. It depends on whether your elimination period is based on calendar days or days of care. If it were based on days of care in this example, it would actually take ten weeks – two and a half months – before the 30-day elimination period would be satisfied.

Coverage Period

Coverage Period refers to how long the insurance will pay once it starts. In the early days of LTC, most everyone offered primarily unlimited lifetime coverage. When the insurance companies figured out that the cost was scaring a lot of people away, they came up with term coverage. Lifetime pays costs for however long a person needs and may be beneficial in cases of dementia where a person is physically healthy but mentally unable to live alone. Dementia cases can last a long time.

☞ CAN YOU IMAGINE: ☜
LTC "What If" Exercise

Frank and Carolyn are in their mid 60s. They both owned term insurance that would expire when they reached their early 70s and they had purchased long-term care insurance. They felt like their term insurance would expire long before they did. Most does. As they reviewed their expenses they realized that their combined costs for various insurance was by far their largest expense. They asked for help.

Keep in mind, this is a specific example and won't be true for many people. It's just that it was for them. They had cheap term insurance and a popular long-term care policy. Frank kept coming back to the same thing that was bothering him. What if he and his wife didn't die in eight years and what if they didn't end up needing much or any of the long-term care? He had a gnawing feeling that he was wasting money that he'd rather see go to his kids and grandkids.

Their financial advisor was able to go through a number of "what if" scenarios and here is what it came down to for them. They were better off financially keeping what they had - their term insurance and their long-term care - as long as they both became disabled within four years and died within eight years. They acknowledged anything can happen, but they were both extremely healthy.

What they opted for was a permanent, guaranteed no-lapse life policy with a long-term care rider. They don't have to worry about premium increases in the long-term care and they know, even if they live to be 120 years old that they or someone they love will get out more money than they put in.

The average nursing home stay is about two and a half years, so if you have three or four-year term, that may cover a significant portion of your risk and help keep the cost down.

Benefit Amount

The benefit amount is simply the amount the company will pay you each day or each month you need the coverage. Typically you will be able to get coverage for between $100 and $500 per day.

Riders

Let's just say there are a confusing number of choices when it comes to riders. My suggestion is to find a good professional who can help you and structure a program to fit your concerns, needs and budget.

One of the basic riders you may want to consider, however, is the inflation rider. It works like this: suppose you decide you want a policy that will pay $150 per day with a 5% compound inflation rider. If you need care in the first year it will pay $150 per day. If you need coverage the next year it will pay $150 plus 5% or $157.50. The next year it goes up 5% and so on.

◀◀◆ WHAT DAD SAID ◆▶▶

You Make Your Money By Buying Right

When it comes to making an investment, you make your money by buying right. Whether you're buying a piece of property or a company's stock, there's no substitute for buying at the right price. There's no antidote for paying too much. Dad used to say, "you make your money on the front end."

The same holds true for LTC. Shop around, ask questions, make sure you understand how all of the moving parts work together before you buy. Make certain you talk with a qualified wealth management or long-term care specialist to determine what you qualify for and the smartest strategy for you.

Alternatives

When long-term care coverage first came out the only thing that was sold was a benefit that would cover you for life no matter how long you needed it. Recently, in order to make it more affordable, many companies have started offering "term" long-term care. Unlike term life insurance, the coverage is yours as long as you continue to pay the premiums. Should you get sick and need the coverage it will pay the benefit amount for a predetermined amount of time – the term. So if you have long-term care with a three year term and 15 years from now you need help, it will pay the benefit amount for three years. This allows the insurance company to substantially lower the price because they are better able to manage their risk. Typical term periods are 3, 4, 5, 7, and 10 years.

There may be other options available to you. One option that has recently come about is the modification of life insurance to cover Long Term Care costs. In most cases it works like this: should you become sick or disabled, you receive a percentage of the face amount (the death benefit) of the life insurance each month until you stop needing it or until the face amount runs out. Whatever you don't use is there for your heirs. Keep in mind that life insurance proceeds are income tax free.

For example, suppose a 65-year old man decides he wants a $150,000 life insurance policy guaranteed not to lapse through age 120 and that it will cost him about $4,500 per year. There are basically three ways someone can get the $150,000. He can die in which case his beneficiary will receive the $150,000 income tax-free (life insurance proceeds are exempt from income taxation). He can become terminally ill, in which case he can start spending the death benefit while he lives. Or he can become disabled – in other words he needs long term care – and begin receiving 2% of the face value, $3,000 per month, income tax-free. Should he pass away before spending the face amount, his beneficiaries will receive the remainder.

Break-Even Analysis

When you are considering the alternatives, don't hesitate to ask for a break-even analysis. This report will show you examples to illustrate if you pay into the policy for five years and then need the benefit, how many days it takes until you've gotten back what you paid into the policy.

Make certain you talk with a qualified wealth management or long-term care specialist to determine what you qualify for and the smartest strategy for you. For you, it may be to self-insure or it may make sense to reinsure to spread the risk around just like you do on your homeowners insurance. That way you can pay pennies on the dollar to reduce or eliminate the potentially debilitating financial effects of a catastrophic health care event.

SUMMING IT UP

o   The chances are good that at least one spouse in a Boomer couple
    will need long term care insurance.

o   There are only two options for payng for long term care: self-insure
    or reinsure. Because of the high costs of care, self insuring is not an
    option for most Boomers.

o   LTC insurance can be made more affordable by adjusting the four
    main components: 1) Elimination period, 2) Coverage period,
    3) Benefit amount and 4) Riders.

1 - Long Term Care, Knowing the Risk, Health Insurance Association of America 1997

2 - Time Magazine, 8/30/1999

3 - Morning Star, Wilmington, NC, 8/22/1996

4 - Planning for Long Term Care, United Seniors Health Council, Washington, DC, McGraw Hill, 2002

5 - Health Policy Institute, Georgetown University, analysis of data from the 2000 National Health Interview Survey, and A. Jones, "The National Nursing Home Survey: 1999 Summary," Vital Health Statistics 13 (152) (2002)

6 - State-Assisted Living Policy: 2000, Mollica, R., national Academy for State Health Policy, Portland, ME

7 - The National Nursing Home Survey: 1999 Summary, National Center for Health Statistics, U.S. Department of Health and Human Services, June 2002

8 - Health Policy Institute, Georgetown University, analysis of data from the 2000 National Health Interview Survey, and A. Jones, "The National Nursing Home Survey: 1999 Summary," Vital Health Statistics 13 (152) (2002)

9 - Cohen, Marc A., Ph.D. & Weinrobe, Maurice, Ph.D., Tax Deductibility of Long Term Care Insurance Premiums, 3/1/2000

Chapter 7
THE OSTRICH SYNDROME

Understanding The Need to Begin Planning Now

If someone you know was inadvertently making a financial mistake that was costing them and their family a few dollars today and thousands of dollars of potential future earnings on those dollars, would you want to tell them? Would you help them?

If you were unintentionally making a financial mistake that was costing your family thousands of dollars every year, when would you want to know about it? If what you believed to be true about part of your finances was wrong, when should you find out? You'd want to know right away, wouldn't you?

If your affairs were arranged by default – if you are using Uncle Sam's estate plan and being lulled into thinking you don't need to do anything about it – would you want to know if your money was not going to pass to your intended recipients? If you could potentially increase what you will leave to your beneficiaries by 30%, 60% or even 100%, would you want to know about it?

Most of us would want to know these things immediately. It's much cheaper to fix something before it becomes a problem – to do it right the first time. Unfortunately, many people put their heads in the sand like an ostrich, without even knowing what they are missing. Sometimes it's not the things we do, it's the things we don't do that hold us back. I did it for years. I didn't

---

✓ **RETIREMENT REALITY CHECK**

Decisive Action
Change is hard. We can't bury our heads in the sand to hide from change. But many people try. Just as technological changes have made us safer on our highways, new technology has the potential to make us safer in our investment strategies. Things that just weren't possible financially a few decades or even a few years ago are possible today. Just as it would be a risky proposition to deny that you need a three-point safety harness (seatbelt) and airbags, it is risky to place our heads in the sand while managing our money in retirement.

It's Like This

IF IT AIN'T BROKE YOU MAY NEED TO CHECK IT OUT ANYWAY

Once upon a time I was 17 years old. I was indestructible. It, whatever "it" was, would never happen to me. "It" almost did.

On a late spring morning in 2004 (no longer 17, I might add), I was driving to a 6:45 a.m. meeting at the Vanderbilt University Club. I drove north on I-65, took the exit at Wedgewood, crossed over 21st Avenue and took a right on Garland. I turned into the parking lot and then turned the wheel slightly to the left to get lined up to pull into the parking space. I thought I had hit ice. My steering didn't respond. I slammed on the brakes - fortunately I was only going about 5 mph. I got out, walked around the truck and looked. I knew it was at least 40 degrees too warm for ice, but that's what it felt like. I got back in and tried to turn into a parking space again. That's when I realized that the steering wheel was freewheeling. There was no connection between it and the front wheels. The steering linkage was completely gone.

It was at that point I realized a couple of things. First, I had to figure out all the details - where to get the truck towed, how to keep anyone from having a collision with it, how to get to my next appointment, how to pick my daughter up that afternoon. You get the picture. More importantly, I realized a miracle had just happened.

As I walked toward the door for my meeting my legs began to shake as my mind raced through a mental video of what would've happened had the steering gone out 5, 10, 20, 50 miles earlier. My son or my daughter might have been in the truck with me. Both had been 48 hours before. I thought where I had driven the last 48 hours: I-40, I-65, Hobson Pike. I thought of the oncoming traffic, the ditches on either side of the road, the guardrails, the corners, and bridges. I had a lot to be thankful for - I was alive, no one else was hurt and my kids weren't in the truck with me.

As the meeting prepared to start, someone asked me about the way I parked. As I told him, he responded, "How inconvenient. That stinks." I suppose you could look at it that way. But I couldn't.

A miracle had just happened: I was alive. I'd get to hold my wife in my arms again. I'd get to see my son take his first steps and hear him say his first words. I'd get to see my daughter start 5th grade. I thought of a thousand things I was thankful for.

It only took me 41 years to come to the realization that my father has been teaching me by example all my life. Regardless of the situation, there are always things to be thankful for. And miracles do happen. I hope you recognize the miracles going on around you.

So what does this have to do with financial planning or money? For me there was a lesson on another level. Most problems start long before the results are realized. The straw that broke the camel's back wasn't the problem and it didn't look like there was any kind of problem before the extra straw was added. Just one straw.

It wasn't broke, so why fix it? With every mile I had been driving, the steering linkage was wearing. As I drove, I thought, "Everything is fine." If a mechanic had called and suggested I come in for a check up, I wouldn't have had the time. Everything was fine. It seemed like the problem showed up all at once.

I hope you're not driving your financial lives in the very same way. The linkage is wearing imperceptibly every day.

know what I didn't know. After all, no one makes financial mistakes on purpose. We make mistakes because of what they don't know. Or because what we "know" that isn't necessarily so. Congratulations to you. The fact that you're reading this tells me you aren't that kind of person. You're the kind that can look at what you're doing and be open to adjusting to new knowledge.

Ch-Ch-Changes

Ever noticed how much we hate change? Do you know someone who wears their hair the same way they did 25 years ago? Do you know someone who dresses in the fashion of a by-gone era? I do. In fact I still wear the same style of blue jeans and loafers I did when I was in high school. On some level I think we all like things to stay the same. But they don't.

If you pulled a Rip Van Winkle and fell asleep sixty years ago and woke up today, it's hard to image how different life has become. If you fell asleep in 1945 and woke up this morning, you woke up to an America with twice as many people and more than 1,000 times more national debt. You fell asleep in a day before faxes, Frisbees, heart transplants, by-pass surgery, pantyhose, ballpoint pens and yogurt. When you fell asleep a nickel would send a first class letter and two postcards – all on the same nickel. You fell asleep at a time when "bunnies" were small rabbits and Rabbits weren't cars. Closets were something you put clothes into, not something people came out of. You could have gone into a five and dime and actually bought stuff for a nickel or a dime. For a nickel you could make a phone call or buy a Pepsi. It was a time before nursing homes, credit cards, smoothies, the Internet, fast food and men with earrings. Timesharing meant spending time together and had nothing to do with computers or real estate. You never thought of "Googling" anything. Making out only meant how well you did on a test. "Grass" was something you cut, "coke" was a cold beverage and "pot" meant something you cooked in. It was a time when a mouse was a rodent, a chip meant a piece of wood, hardware meant hardware and software wasn't even a word yet. Things have changed.

You could've bought a new Chevy coupe for about $600, but who could afford one at that price! That's too bad because gas was just $.11 a gallon. Good thing it was cheap because no one really thought about fuel economy.

But times changed and technology changed. The automobile you bought in 1945 had higher polluting emissions, less horsepower and a larger engine than today's comparable car. That 1945 auto didn't have crumple zones, antilock brakes, front airbags, side-impact airbags or even a seat belt. You had to wait around till about 1957 to get basic, across-the-lap seat belts. Cars today are safer, more fuel-efficient and have fewer lead pollutants being spewed into our air.

What Planning Can Do For You

I have had phone calls from people who have decided they need to start planning for retirement. When asked when they plan on retiring, all too often, the answer is "in a few months" or "a couple of years." Invariably, if they have done this without professional help along the way, I hear "If I had known then what I know now I would have..."

There are ten main areas that good planning can help improve.

1) Having a plan will help you take health care costs into consideration.
2) Having a plan will help you take inflation into consideration.
3) Having a plan will help you take taxes into consideration.
4) Having a plan will keep you from overestimating how much you can withdraw from your retirement nest egg.
5) Having a plan will help you deal with market volatility.
6) Having a plan will help keep you from underestimating expenses in retirement.
7) Having a plan will help keep you from taking too much risk, or the wrong kinds of risk, with your investments.
8) Having a plan will help keep you from underestimating life expectancy.
9) Having a plan will help your family when you're no longer able to care for them.
10) Having a plan will help you have more of a life.

✓   **RETIREMENT REALITY CHECK**   ↖

An estimated 44% of retirees are likely to outlive their retirement savings and 69% of retirees will work well into their 70s.

For Retirees, Savings Might Come Up Short, *USA Today*, Nov. 4, 2003

Let's look at some of the most common pitfalls that can occur by pro-crastinating and doing nothing. By understanding the pitfalls, we can take action to avoid them.

General Oversights

We could call general planning mistakes oversights. These are the things that we know to do but forget because of our busy lives. Someone gets remarried and doesn't change the beneficiary designations on their IRAs or life insurance. Someone has another grandchild and plans are not adjusted to treat each grandchild equally. Someone changes jobs and leaves money in an old 401(k) instead of doing a qualified rollover into an IRA. They forget about the differences, as far as the IRS is concerned, between an IRA and a 401(k).

Or even worse, they keep meaning to get a will or update their will. Sadly, only about 30% of adults in America even have a will.[1]

Increased Costs

With the passage of time, things certainly change. If you have life insurance, this is one of those areas. As you know, people are tending to live longer lives. Because of this, insurance companies have, by and large,

---

☞ CAN YOU IMAGINE: ☜
It's Hard To Let Go

A prospective client came in to visit with an advisor. He had done well growing his money over the years and had accumulated over $2,000,000 in growth companies such as Home Depot, Wal-Mart, and Cracker Barrel. He was retiring and needed an income of about $80,000 per year from his portfolio. He said he was comfortable with what he owned, needed only about 4% income currently and did not want to spend his principal - all seemingly reasonable requirements. He said since he had averaged more than 10% over the past decade he didn't need to make any changes.

He owned some great companies. So the advisor asked him what he was going to sell. Can you see his dilemma? He didn't want to sell anything. He had $2,000,000. But he had no income to speak of. None of the companies he owned paid any substantial dividends.

The only way to get income from his portfolio was to sell something to provide the money to spend.

decreased mortality costs. Do you think your insurance company is ever going to send you a letter saying, "even though you're happy paying the rate you're currently paying, we're going to dramatically reduce your costs"? Don't hold your breath. According to a recent study quoted in *Trust and Estates Magazine,* 75% of life insurance policies more than five years old could have increased their death benefit by 40% without an increase in premium. If you don't ask, you won't know.

New Tools To Manage Risk

Over the past 60 years there have been dramatic improvements in safety standards and technology in the automotive industry. Today we reap those benefits when we buy newer model vehicles.

Likewise, there have been new tools and technologies developed for managing risk in portfolios. It makes sense to be aware of the tools to know if they will help us develop a lifetime of worry-free income.

Distribution Order Mistakes

Not paying attention to your withdrawal options and the tax implications of how your accounts are set up could lead to several avoidable mistakes. The order you withdraw from your accounts can affect the tax status for you and your heirs.

Where should you get your retirement income? Should you withdraw from your tax-deferred accounts first? Or your taxable accounts? Or your tax-free accounts? Changing the withdrawal order can make years of difference in how long your money lasts.

✓   **RETIREMENT REALITY CHECK**   ⌁

Knowledge
"75% of life insurance policies more than five years old could have increased their death benefit by 40% without an increase in premium."

- Trust and Estates Magazine, May 2003

Missed Opportunities Because I Didn't Know They Existed

One of the worst things I get to hear is, "I wish I had known I could…" and one of the neatest things is to show people a strategy and hear them say, "I had no idea I could do that."

Did you know you could withdraw from an IRA or 401(k) before age 59 1/2 *without* a 10% penalty? It's true. If you do it correctly. The Internal Revenue Code is our rulebook. We have to know how to use its provisions for your best advantage. Do you have highly appreciated stock in your retirement account? Did you know there are special provisions for you to help you pay less tax? There are. It's not surprising that most people don't know there's a dramatic difference between IRA and 401(k) provisions – especially when it comes to the options available to your heirs. New rulings on retirement accounts come out from the IRS virtually every week (called "private letter rulings"). So things are constantly changing.

"To My Beloved Government, for Years of Devoted Service, I Hereby Bequeath…"(And Other Simple Mistakes That Can Cost a Lot)

Not only do we need to manage our money in retirement, but we must also make sure those assets are titled properly. Attention to detail will help you control who receives your money after you're gone and will help prepare for a smooth transference of assets. Common mistakes in titling assets (and the problems they cause) can have a profound effect on families for generations.

There are several ways to title and pass on your property. A few of the most common are:

- Joint tenants with right of survivorship
- Tenancy by the entirety
- Tenancy in common
- Sole ownership
- Trust
- Will
- Intestate succession

> *"If you don't love anyone, don't care what becomes of your possessions or don't care about making things easier for the people you leave behind, you don't need a will."*
> — Anonymous

For example, suppose you have assets held under joint tenancy (joint tenants with right of survivorship or JTWROS), you might assume that all of your assets will be disposed of through the instructions of your will. However, assets titled under joint tenancy will, in fact, supercede the will. If you own an annuity, a titling mistake could cost your heirs important tax benefits and potentially a loss of guarantees. Is the annuity owner-driven or annuitant-driven? It can make a huge difference to your heirs. Additionally, beneficiary designations on retirement accounts and annuities actually override the wishes stated in a person's will. Do you have a 401(k)? If so, do you know if your beneficiary designation is *per capita* or *per stirpes?* It's important.

With complexity of current estate tax laws and the sunset provision, it's easy to be lulled into doing nothing. Some folks assume that since they may still be under the estate tax unified credit limits that their estate won't be subject to estate tax. What they may not have taken into account is that their insurance may be owned personally and not by a

---

It's Like This

Don't Lock The Controls

Suppose you want to go on vacation to Miami, Florida. Your airplane leaves the runway headed toward Miami. There has been a flight plan filed, there have been calculations to determine the allowable load, the right amount of fuel and the weather conditions have been determined. After the plane takes off there are constant adjustments to compensate for winds, air temperature differences etc. If the plane lifted off with the course set and no in-flight adjustments were made, even though the plane was pointed in the right direction, chances are slim that it would reach the right city, little less be on target enough to touch down safely on a strip of asphalt a few yards wide.

Yet many people treat their money as though they were putting it on an airplane, pointing it in the right direction and hoping that it lands in the right vicinity. Maybe it doesn't make any difference if the final destination is Detroit instead of Miami. Maybe it does. You decide.

RETIREMENT REALITY CHECK

Realistic Expectations

Our government has "permanently" abolished the estate tax two times before. And then brought it back. The government's definition of "permanent" is different than your and my definition.

trust. While it is true that life insurance proceeds are exempt from income tax, they are not necessarily exempt from estate tax. And some states, Tennessee included, may have an estate tax payable upon the passing of the first spouse.

Planning ahead may avoid costly probate, allow you to control your assets, and addresses the tax implications in a reasonable way.

Estate Taxes

While estate taxes can be astronomical in size and impact, they are part of the "transference" phase and a detailed discussion is beyond the scope of our focus on lifetime income. But they deserve at least a mention.

Don't assume that just because the "marital exclusion" has been going up that you don't need to give any attention to this area. In 2010, the estate tax goes away but will come back in 2011. Make sure you have a professional look under the hood to check things out.

An attorney friend of mine says half jokingly that he hates it when people do estate planning. He says it's much less expensive to avert a problem before it happens than to fix it afterwards. It's much more profitable for him when people have done no planning. I'm sure he's kidding; I think.

☞ CAN YOU IMAGINE: ☜
When You Assume

Bob was in his early 60s and had changed companies several times during his career in hospital management. He had two children and three young grandchildren. When he came to visit a comprehensive planner he still had money in 401(k)s with three previous employers that he hadn't rolled over into IRAs.

No one had explained the differences as far as the IRS is concerned between a 401(k) and an IRA. He had assumed there was no difference. But the IRS doesn't usually grant exceptions because you don't know what the rules are.

Thank goodness he found out and took decisive action based on his knowledge and rolled his 401(k)s into an IRA. His action may have saved his beneficiaries over $170,000.

An Annual Financial Checkup In Retirement

As you move into retirement, it will probably be the first time for you. Retiring is an important event. One you'll want to make sure you're in good form for because when you retire, your responsibility to prudently manage your financial affairs hasn't ended. Just like you get a checkup to make sure your body is working well, it only makes sense to get a checkup on your finances to make sure they are staying healthy.

Do you have a written plan guiding your overall financial decisions? I'm not talking about just a will or a trust. I mean a plan. A trust and a will may be part of the plan, but they're not the plan. Most working class Americans, including those making several hundred thousand dollars per year, don't.

I know, armed with this knowledge, you won't fall into the procrastination trap or the Ostrich Syndrome.

SUMMING IT UP

o   Change is always hard, but Boomers should not let their fear of change prevent them from taking advantage of new technology that helps their investments work harder in retirement.

o   When you tap into your investments, what kind of investments you tap and the order you tap them can dramatically affect how your investments perform.

o   There are ways of saving money that may have been overlooked - and that's where an advanced planner may be able to help.

o   Make it a habit to have an annual financial check up with your financial advisor.

1- Leave A Legacy™

Chapter 8
THE ROAD MAP

Creating the Plan and Its Value to You

When it comes to investing and accumulating money, time is your best friend. When it comes to planning, time is your worst enemy. The old "good book" says, "Tomorrow is promised to no one." And procrastination is one of the deadliest sins when it comes to planning. You are one of the enlightened few; by the virtue of reading this you are investing in your future and taking a meaningful step in the planning process – gaining knowledge.

> *"The man with the average mentality, but with control, with a definite goal, and a clear conception of how it may be gained, and above all, with the power of application and labor, wins in the end."*
>
> —William Howard Taft

When I started as a stockbroker, I had no idea what the possibilities were when it came to helping people improve their lives – and the lives of generations to come – through proper planning. It wasn't that I didn't want to help people; I myopically thought my job was just about helping them get the highest rate of return. Boy, was I wrong. I

✓ | **RETIREMENT REALITY CHECK** | ⌐

Why Should YOU Have A Comprehensive Written Plan?
Simple. Planning can help you address and improve these main areas:
1) Creating wealth
2) Protecting wealth
3) Reducing income taxes
4) Reducing estate taxes
5) Reducing stress
6) Increasing net, after tax income
7) Increasing your likelihood of success, of getting where you want to go
8) Allowing your family to know what to do when life changes (and it will)
9) Increasing the odds of getting what you want when you want it
10) Ensuring that you don't outlive your money

just didn't know what it was that I didn't know. And I was trained "in the business."

One of the most rewarding aspects of what I get to do on a daily basis is helping people arrange their affairs and assets to provide the lifestyle they want and help preserve the assets for generations to come. It's a real joy to see the looks on peoples' faces when we can help them arrange things so they can save thousands of dollars in current and future taxes. Before I started planning I wasn't aware of the dramatic impact small adjustments could make.

When I talk about a plan, let me tell you what I'm not talking about. Some financial service firms, banks and brokerage firms will print off a boilerplate report from "financial planning software" and call it a plan. Have you seen one of those? Many companies print them off for free. Your name is merged into a report with pretty color graphs, pie charts straight line rate of return assumptions and huge disclaimers. I'll confess, in less enlightened previous years, I have even given those to clients. I'm embarrassed now when I think about all the trees killed for such a pointless exercise.

When I talk about a plan, what I am talking about is a comprehensive financial plan customized to your specific life situation as it is today and as you want it to be in the future. It's like the difference between reading information on the internet and being diagnosed by your family physician. If you were seriously concerned about your physical health, you'd see a professional rather than just visit a web site. The same applies to your financial health.

Your Investment Plan

When it comes to reaching your financial dreams and goals, the common denominator is having enough money to fully fund whatever it is that you want or need.

In my years of helping folks do exactly that, I have yet to see anyone make a financial mistake on purpose. They simply make financial mistakes because of what they don't understand. It is easy to see how this can happen when you consider the process most working Americans have endured in seeking sound financial advice. The bank tells you one thing, the CPA another, the insurance agent another, the stockbroker another and next thing you know you end up with a mess. Can you see how this would create a willy-nilly planning situation?

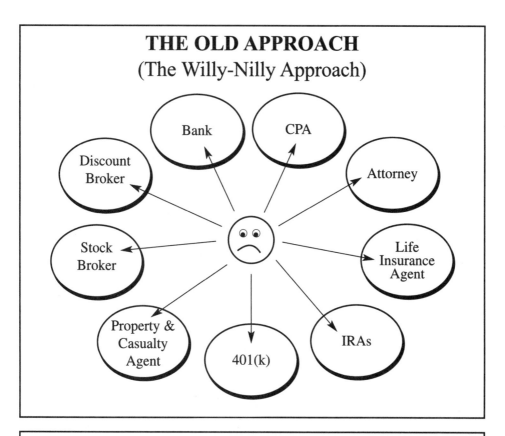

THE OLD APPROACH
(The Willy-Nilly Approach)

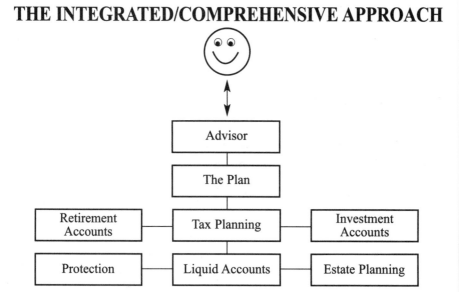

THE INTEGRATED/COMPREHENSIVE APPROACH

The Plan is a Road Map

Imagine you live in Nashville, Tennessee and want to take a vacation to San Diego, California. Would you consider using a map? Of course you would. Shouldn't we give more attention and spend more time planning for rest-of-our-life income than we give to our next vacation? If you take off on that trip at 70 miles per hour, hit all the lights green and avoid all traffic jams, you'll never get to San Diego if you're headed in the wrong direction. If you break every rate of return record in the history of the world you will still have failed if you don't get to your desired destination.

Having a road map won't keep detours or snowstorms from happening, but it will give you a reasonable way to deal with the unexpected. A good road map gives you alternatives to still arrive at your destination.

When the engineers of the Titanic claimed they had built the unsinkable ship, they didn't add that it was unsinkable as long as it didn't hit an iceberg on the starboard side. We need to make sure we plan our financial lives so the hull is strong - but we also need to make sure we have plenty of life rafts.

> *"If you don't know where you're going, you'll probably end up somewhere else."*
> — Anonymous

One other thought on having a comprehensive written plan. If it's just in your head it's really more of a thought than an actual plan. And there is a difference. Commit it to paper. There is power in having it in writing.

Successful People Use Coaches

Even if you're not a sports fan, the names Tiger Woods, Lance Armstrong and Muhammad Ali probably ring a bell. These three men are

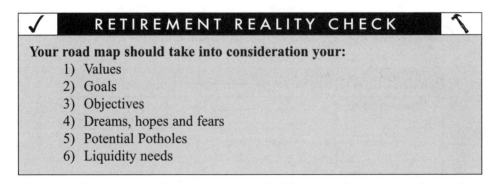

✓ **RETIREMENT REALITY CHECK** ↖

Your road map should take into consideration your:
1) Values
2) Goals
3) Objectives
4) Dreams, hopes and fears
5) Potential Potholes
6) Liquidity needs

highly talented athletes. Their minds and bodies worked together in ways that defy what seems humanly possible – all three exhibited brilliant abilities. But even if you are a sports fan, you may not recognize the names Butch Harmon, Chris Carmichael and Joe Martin – the coaches, respectively, of Wood, Armstrong and Ali. Did you ever wonder why such exceptionally talented athletes need a coach? Butch Harmon didn't win tournaments like Tiger. Chris didn't win the Tour De France even once. Joe Martin never came close to boxing like Cassius Clay. And yet these men had coaches.

These athletes use a coach to help them formulate a training plan and stay on track. A financial advisor should do the same for you. He or she should help bring out the best in you to help you make the decisions that will help you end up with the life you want.

You probably haven't retired before. Just about anything is hard if you've never done it. The first time you tried to ride a bike was difficult. Doesn't it make sense to get help from someone who's gone through the retirement transition hundreds of times? Retiring is not something you want to have to ask for a "do over." Wouldn't you agree it's important to get it right the first time?

Hire A Pro

The first step toward having a good financial roadmap is to hire a qualified professional that can help make all the pieces work together. The wealthiest Americans hire good advisors and I think you should, too. Given the complexities of investments and the related tax laws it's a smart decision. I know some people think they can read a few books and do it on their own, but then again some people think they can read a couple of books and do their own brain surgery.

When considering hiring a professional to help you, the most important considerations are finding someone you trust, someone that knows what to do

✓ RETIREMENT REALITY CHECK ↖

48% of Boomer retirees will be below poverty line without social security.

Fast Facts and Figures, Social Security Administration, 2001

and will follow through and do it. If the trust element is not there, there's no need to waste your time.

You should find someone who will always place your interests first. Someone who will tell you – and be willing to testify in a court of law – what a prudent person would do in your situation. You'll need someone who will always tell you the truth – good news or bad.

To find a good financial coach, you should interview them, just as you would (or should) with any other professional, like your physician, attorney and CPA. During your initial consultation with a planning professional, discuss your values, concerns or even fears, as well as your financial goals and objectives. You should have available your account statements, insurance information and tax returns for the past year or two.

What should you look for? Beyond the first critical elements of trust, integrity and competency there are a few other items you'll want to look for.

1) You may want to deal with someone that has a **team**, not just a sole practitioner. That way, you'll leverage the different strengths and talents of a team of people working on your behalf.

2) You'll probably want to know what their process is for monitoring your account – in other words, how will you know someone's **"watching the store."**

3) You'll also want to know **how they get paid**. Are they paid on commission or is their compensation tied in some way to the performance of your account? Most of us know that when we pay commissions, the advisor's compensation is divorced from your results. I can honestly say every advisor I have ever known has wanted their clients to do well. Working with one that is paid on some sort of an asset-based fee inextricably marries the advisor's compensation to the client's results. Many people like that arrange-

---

✓ **RETIREMENT REALITY CHECK** ⟍

Three main questions to consider in selecting a financial advisor:
1) Can I trust you?
2) Do I think you know what you're doing?
3) Will you do it?

ment. It keeps the monetary motivations very straight forward: if the client makes money, the advisor's fee goes up; if the client loses money, the advisor's fee goes down.

4) You may want to know what they are **able to sell**. Everyone that calls themselves some flavor of financial advisor should be licensed. If someone is very limited in what they can recommend, you may get advice that is limited. This may help you understand some of the most common licenses. If they have a:

✐ CAN YOU IMAGINE: ✎
Income Silos

Mike was 57 years old and had been retired since he sold his company 10 years earlier. Due to some market losses he had experienced he was nervous about being able to maintain his income so he sought out a comprehensive financial planner.

There would have to be some hard decisions made. He needed an 8-9% income and was heavily invested in bonds for income but they were yielding 4 1/2 - 6%. To get the income he needed required a withdrawal rate that was not in the safe range. The advisor figured out a way to increase the likelihood Mike could get the result he wanted but knew on first blush it was going to sound like the wrong prescription.

The advisor suggested Mike set up "income silos." If you've ever traveled through rural parts of the mid-west you've seen a series of silos set up by train tracks. They set up three silos for his portfolio. The plan was to have two income silos and have the third silo be a growth silo.

Silo one would be populated with investment instruments that pay interest and are liquidated so Mike would spend not only the interest but also the principal in silo one. In 10 years his principal and interest would be completely depleted and silo one would be completely empty. I know that sounds like a prescription for going broke and that's what Mike thought. But he listened for the rest of the story.

Silo two was to be set up for income with the plan that the principal would not be touched.

The key for Mike was what happens with silo three. It would be set up for growth with everything reinvested and give it time to grow without putting strain on the silo three investments for ten years. What he did with silo one allowed silo three to be set up for growth.

Mike realized that the key to getting what he wanted was to use a process that was very counter-intuitive to him initially.

a) Series 6 – they are registered to recommend "packaged products"

b) Series 7 – they are registered to recommend individual securities and packaged products

c) Series 65 or 66 – they are registered as a Registered Investment Advisor representative so they can charge an asset management fee

d) Insurance license – they are licensed to recommend fixed insurance products. (Variable insurance products require an insurance license and a securities registration).

5) You may want to know if they work for a firm with proprietary products, if they are limited mainly to products from one firm or if they are **independent.**

6) You'll probably want to know how they work, their investment **philosophy**, do they specialize in something, do they **specialize** in working with certain kind of people and are they comprehensive in their planning.

One Size Doesn't Fit All

Let's face it, there is a dizzying array of choices today. And a slew of places you can go to own them. With ever-increasing specialization there are a lot of great products, programs and methods available today. The key is using the specialized tools in the appropriate situation and the advisor should always be the client's advocate to make that happen.

The "one size fits all" approach comes in many flavors. First there is the "insurance is the answer to every need you have" approach. Need to retire, educate your children, and have money to buy a car? "Insurance will do all that and walk your dog." Then there is the stockbroker answer, which goes something like "I don't do insurance because... I have a system for picking great stocks and I get a return of at least..." Another variation is the "I specialize in this type of investment because they always..." Still another is, "my new firm's research is so much better than my last firm's research." You'll want to find someone who focuses on what you want and need, not on what they want to sell.

There are a number of good investment vehicles available. But any vehicle, misapplied, will yield poor or at least unintended results. When things are going along swimmingly there is a tendency for us to get complacent. After all, a rising tide lifts all ships, but it's not until the tide goes back out that you see who is truly sea worthy. You'll probably want someone who isn't tied to just one firm's product.

When you get into the numbers, there are four areas of your financial life that need to fit together. I have yet to see any two people where these four areas are identical.

FOUR AREAS OF YOUR FINANCIAL LIFE	
CASH (Liquidity for Emergencies)	**GROWTH** (Your Hedge Against Rising Costs)
INCOME (Steady Cash Flow Investments)	**PROTECTION** (Health, Auto, Life, Disability Protection)

You'll want to have a plan that you understand, are comfortable with and addresses the inevitabilities of inflation and increasing life expectancy. It should deal specifically with your needs for liquidity, income and protection. It should help you deal with the emotional cycle of investing and protect you from having to cash-in fluctuating investments in a compressed market. And it should help you arrange things in a way that you and the people you love minimize tax expenses.

Creating Your Map in Five Simple Steps

Your financial professional should be able to help you in a simple five-step process.

1) **Identify and define** what you want out of life: your investment objectives, goals and dreams.

2) Determine your personal **risk tolerance** and **investment time frame**

3) **Develop a strategy** - create a personalized financial strategy for you including diversification plans, tactical considerations, tax strategies, investment policy, manager selection process

4) **Implement your plan** using appropriate strategies and tactics consistent with your philosophy and investment policy statement

5) **Monitor** progress toward your destination and make **adjustments** as appropriate

Of course after you have the plan, you'll want to review it annually with your advisor to update it with any changes that have happened in your family or in your life and make certain that other changes, like tax laws, haven't created the need for any revisions. Call it an in-flight adjustment.

To make things easier for you, at the end of this book is an Action Plan

It's Like This

Building A House

Building a portfolio is like building a house. If you don't get the foundation poured correctly, it doesn't matter how much time you spend picking out beautiful paint colors for the walls. You'd have crooked walls, uneven floors and corners that aren't square.

with a "To Do" list to help you get the process started. There is also a section on selecting an advisor to help you with appropriate questions and the answers you should expect. Finally, there is a list of questions that you (and your advisor) should be able to answer about your plan.

Conclusion

Every good sermon has an invitation, an alter call. And here it is: here we stand, faced with the prospect of living longer lives and having to deal with the realities of inflation for longer periods. Most of us don't have company pensions to rely upon, so we have to shoulder the risk of generating income that will last throughout our lives. Social Security is facing inevitable reform. Taxes don't go away. The rules keep getting more complex.

The good news is that you can plan, you can achieve. To that end, I've included some resources in the back of this book to help you get started on your plan and on a journey to a better financial life for you and your loved ones. It's not

◄► WHAT DAD SAID ◄►

What Really Matters

By the time I was 17, I had been working for a few years mowing yards, working in my dad's car business in the summers and teaching guitar lessons at two music stores. I had saved up a little money. My dad had this way of asking questions where it sounded like you had a choice. So he gave me a choice. He said I could put my money in the bank or I could put it in the bank, that is, invest in the bank. Either way, I was going to put money into savings. There was a new local bank in formation and he suggested I take some of my money and invest in bank stock. Truth is, I didn't really have much choice.

Discipline is never much fun when you're the one to which it's being applied. But am I ever glad he made me understand the importance of not spending that money, but using it to plant a seed. A few years later Liberty National of Louisville bought out the Bank of Elizabethtown and a few years after that Bank One of Cincinnati, Ohio bought out Liberty and then JP Morgan bought out Bank One.

A few years after planting that seed I was able to use part of the money I made on that stock to buy my first piece of investment real estate.

enough to have information and hope. We must have knowledge and take action.

I hope this helps you be better prepared for a wonderful life today and for many decades to come! Enjoy the journey!

SUMMING IT UP

o   Boomers must have a comprehensive, written retirement plan if they hope to attain their financial goals.

o   Capable people use coaches to keep them on track. Find and make use of an experienced financial advisor.

o   A good plan is about more than money - it's about how to attain your lifetime goals.

Appendix

Action "To Do" List

• Read this book

• Take notes of your questions, concerns, goals, wishes

• Gather statements from:
    o Bank
    o Investment firms
    o Mutual funds
    o Annuities
    o IRAs
    o 401(k)

• Set appointment with advisor

• Get a plan tailored to help you get what you want

• Implement your plan

• Live!

Your First Planning Meeting

Your financial professional should be able to help you in a simple
five-step process.

1) **Identify and define** what you want out of life: your investment
   objectives, goals and dreams.

2) Determine your personal **risk tolerance** and **investment time
   frame**

3) **Develop a strategy** - create a personalized financial strategy for
   you including diversification plans, tactical considerations, tax
   strategies, investment policy, manager selection process

4) **Implement your plan** using appropriate strategies and tactics
   consistent with your philosophy and investment policy statement

5) **Monitor** progress toward your destination and make **adjustments**
   as appropriate

Selecting An Advisor

What should you look for? Beyond the first critical elements of **trust, integrity** and **competency** there are a few other items you'll want to look for.

1) You may want to deal with someone that has a team, not just a sole practitioner. That way, you'll leverage the different strengths and talents of a **team** of people working on your behalf.

2) You'll probably want to know what their process is for monitoring your account – in other words, how will you know someone's **"watching the store."** How often are review meetings? How often and why will they call?

3) You'll also want to know **how they get paid.** Are they paid on commission or is their compensation tied in some way to the performance of your account? Most of us know that when we pay commissions, the advisor's compensation is divorced from your results. I can honestly say every advisor I have ever known has wanted their clients to do well. Working with one that is paid on some sort of an asset-based fee inextricably marries the advisor's compensation to the client's results. Many people like that arrangement. It keeps the monetary motivations very straight forward: if the client makes money, the advisor's fee goes up; if the client loses money, the advisor's fee goes down.

4) You may want to know what they are **able to sell**. Everyone that calls themselves some flavor of financial advisor should be licensed. If someone is very limited in what they can recommend, you may get advice that is limited. This may help you understand some of the most common licenses. If they have a:

   a) Series 6 – they are registered to recommend "packaged products"
   b) Series 7 – they are registered to recommend individual securities and packaged products

    c) Series 65 or 66 – they are registered as a Registered Investment Advisor representative so they can charge an asset management fee

    d) Insurance license – they are licensed to recommend fixed insurance products. (Variable insurance products require an insurance license and a securities registration).

5) You may want to know if they work for a firm with proprietary products, if they are limited mainly to products from one firm or if they are **independent**.

6) You'll probably want to know how they work, their investment **philosophy**, do they specialize in something, do they **specialize** in working with certain kind of people and are they **comprehensive** in their planning (if they do not require and review tax returns and statements, the planning is not comprehensive).

Questions To Ask Yourself About Your Plan

These are the basic questions and scenarios a good plan should address. A plan that doesn't address all of these items is not really a plan but a hope. We should each know – and be comfortable with – the answers to these basic items.

- What happens if I live longer than I expect?
    - o Is my money likely to last?
    - o What if I physically can't work in retirement?

- What happens if I don't live as long as I expect?
    - o What will happen to the people who depend on me?
    - o Do they know what to do?
    - o Who will they get answers from?
    - o Have I prepared them?
    - o Will they get the money I want them to get?
        - – When I want them to get it?
        - – How I want them to get it?

- What if inflation goes up or down?
    - o Do I have assets that are likely to benefit?

- What if "the market" goes up or down?
    - o Do I have money that is likely to benefit?
    - o Do I have a strategy and a plan if the market goes up more than I expect?
    - o Do I have a strategy and a plan if the market goes down more than I expect?

- Do I have a strategy for knowing when tax law changes affect me?

- What if an emergency arises?
    - o Do I have the funds to cover it?
    - o Can I cover it without cashing in investments that may be down?

- What happens if I'm disabled before I retire?

- What happens if I'm disabled after I retire?

FINANCIAL OVERVIEW

This is a data gathering form, providing the fundamental details on which a financial overview may be built. Items in this form are essential to the completion of a financial analysis. Please print clearly, leaving blank any answers you are unsure about. It is OK to estimate dollar amounts. When you submit this form please include:

- Copy of your most recent tax return
- Investment account statements
- Annuity contracts and last statement
- Life insurance policies and last statement

Date _____ / _____ / _____

Name _____

Nickname _____

Spouse/
Partner's Name _____

Nickname _____

Mailing Address _____

City _____

State _____ Zip _____

Home Phone _____

E-mail Address _____

Employer _____

Occupation _____

Work Phone _____ Salary _____

Date of Birth _____ Social Security # _____

Spouse/Partner Employer _____

Occupation _____

Work Phone _____ Salary _____

Date of Birth _____ Social Security # _____

Are you eligible to participate in an employer-sponsored retirement plan?

      Head of the Household: Yes_____No_____

      Spouse/Partner: Yes_____No_____

Are you concerned about possible long-term care expenses?

      Yes_____No_____

Checking, Savings and Money Market (Non-IRA) Accounts

NAME OF INSTITUTION	TYPE OF ACCOUNT	MATURITY DATE	INTEREST RATE	APPROX. BALANCE
			%	$
			%	$
			%	$

IRAs and Other Retirement Accounts

TYPE (401k, IRA, TSA, etc.)	LOCATION (Bank, Broker, Employer)	APPROXIMATE MARKET VALUE
		$
		$
		$
		$

Stocks and Bonds (in which you hold the certificate)

NAME OF STOCK/ BOND	NUMBER OF SHARES	APPROXIMATE MARKET VALUE
		$
		$
		$
		$

Mutual Funds and/or Brokerage Accounts

NAME OF MUTUAL FUND OR BROKERAGE ACCT.	NUMBER OF SHARES	APPROXIMATE MARKET VALUE
		$
		$
		$
		$

Annuities

Company #1 _____

Annuitant/Owner _____

Interest Rate _____ %   Fixed or Variable _____

Contract Date _____   Approx. Market Value $_____

Company #2 _____

Annuitant/Owner _____

Interest Rate _____ %   Fixed or Variable _____

Contract Date _____   Approx. Market Value $_____

Company #3 _____

Annuitant/Owner _____

Interest Rate _____ %   Fixed or Variable _____

Contract Date _____   Approx. Market Value $_____

Life Insurance

COMPANY	NAME OF INSURED	TYPE (Whole Life, Term, etc.)	APPROXIMATE DEATH BENEFIT	CASH VALUE
_____	_____	_____	$_____	$_____
_____	_____	_____	$_____	$_____
_____	_____	_____	$_____	$_____
_____	_____	_____	$_____	$_____

Real Estate Portfolio Detail

(Please use the following abbreviations for type:

PR = Primary Residence   SR = Secondary Residence   R = Recreation Property

F = First Mortgage   I = Investment Property   O = Other

TYPE	MARKET VALUE	EQUITY	TERM (Years)	MORTGAGE BALANCE	MONTHLY PAYMENT	INTEREST RATE
_____	$_____	$_____	_____	$_____	$_____	____%
_____	$_____	$_____	_____	$_____	$_____	____%
_____	$_____	$_____	_____	$_____	$_____	____%
_____	$_____	$_____	_____	$_____	$_____	____%

Liabilities

(Please do not include real estate loans in this section.)

ITEM/ COMPANY NAME	BALANCE	MINIMUM PAYMENT	CURRENT PAYMENT	INTEREST RATE
Auto Loan 1: _____	$_____	$_____	$_____	____%
Auto Loan 2: _____	$_____	$_____	$_____	____%
Auto Loan 3: _____	$_____	$_____	$_____	____%
Rec. Vehicle: _____	$_____	$_____	$_____	____%
Credit Card: _____	$_____	$_____	$_____	____%
Credit Card: _____	$_____	$_____	$_____	____%
Credit Card: _____	$_____	$_____	$_____	____%
Line of Credit: _____	$_____	$_____	$_____	____%
Student Loan: _____	$_____	$_____	$_____	____%
Other: _____	$_____	$_____	$_____	____%

Household Cash Flow

HEAD OF THE HOUSEHOLD WAGES: $_____/Year
Source: _____

SPOUSE/PARTNER WAGES: $_____/Year
Source: _____

OTHER INCOME: $_____/Year
Source: _____

OTHER INCOME: $_____/Year
Source: _____

How much can you afford to save each month, including what you are saving now? $_____

What are your approximate annual expenses? $_____

General Questions

What are your primary financial concerns? (Please list in order of importance.)

_____

_____

What are your retirement expectations?

	Desired Monthly Retirement Income	Assumed Rate of Inflation	Retirement Age
HEAD OF THE HOUSEHOLD:	$_____	_____%	_____
SPOUSE/PARTNER:	$_____	_____%	_____

Do you have any Wills?   Yes_____   No_____
If yes, when drafted? _____
Do you have any Trusts?   Yes_____   No_____
If yes, when drafted? _____
Please add any additional information you would like to share with us.

_____

_____

How to Ruin Your Retirement

- Assume everything is fine the way it is

- Assume you'll live to only to your life expectancy

- Pay taxes you don't have to pay

- Make decisions based only on your hatred of taxes

- Leave your 401(k) at your former employer

- Ignore the consequences of taxes

- Invest emotionally

- Don't plan for liquidity needs

- Don't be concerned about expenses

- Make decisions based only on expenses

- Use a willy-nilly approach, don't have a plan

- Assume "it" will never happen to you

- Invest too aggressively

- Invest too conservatively

- Don't get an annual financial check-up in retirement

- Don't diversify

- Don't use tax diversification

- Don't consider your risk

- Don't hire a team – do your own tax work

- Don't hire a team – do your own investment work

- Don't hire a team – do your own legal work

- Believe past performance really IS a guarantee of future performance

Recommended Reading

The Automatic Millionaire, David Bach

The Retirement Savings Time Bomb and How To Defuse It, Ed Slott

Smart Women Finish Rich, David Bach

The Next Great Bubble Boom, Harry Dent

The Great Boom Ahead, Harry Dent

Age Power, Ken Dychtwald

Reminescences of a Stock Operator, Edwin LeFevre

Values-Based Financial Planning, the Art of Creating an Inspiring Financial Strategy, Bill Bachrach

NOTES

NOTES

NOTES

NOTES

NOTES

NOTES